PUBLISHED BY:
**Àmbit Serveis Editorials, S.A.**
Consell de Cent, 282, Entresòl, 2ª
08007 Barcelona. Tel. 34 93 488 01 50

© 1999, edition:
**Daura Foundation**

TEXTS:
© Teresa Macià
   Pilar Vélez
   Francesc Fontbona

TRANSLATION FROM THE CATALAN:
Elaine Fradley et al.

PHOTOGRAPHS:
© Daura Archives and the photographers

DL: B-39712-1999
ISBN: 84-89681-36-8

# Pierre Daura

## ( 1896 - 1976 )

TERESA MACIÀ

PILAR VÉLEZ
*prologue*

FRANCESC FONTBONA
*epilogue*

àmbit

# CONTENTS

# THE REDISCOVERY OF PIERRE DAURA

Pilar Vélez

Some books are definitive, and some lead to other projects which turn out to be definitive — if we accept that anything is ever final, particularly in the study and interpretation of works of art. Nonetheless, in the attempt to sketch out an artist's career, his points of reference and his convictions, there are certain steps we have to take. This book by Teresa Macià on the Catalan, French and American painter, Pierre Daura, is the first step in the analysis of this artist, carried out by a person who has become the foremost authority on his work. This is not only because of her research, which is always necessary, but also because of her personal involvement in the rediscovery and publicizing of the artist, in close collaboration with Martha Daura, the painter's daughter.

The rediscovery of an artist can be the consequence of a variety of events. Sometimes, the sudden influx into the market of a large volume of work brings him to the fore in an unexpected way, especially if his work has remained exclusively in the hands of the family for years after his death. In other cases, a commemoration (centenary of his birth, fiftieth anniversary of his death…) prompts public cultural institutions to pay tribute to him and to organize a comprehensive exhibition with an appropriate catalogue. Or, perhaps a young art historian, under the guidance of an enlightened professor or specialist, chooses him as the subject of a doctoral thesis, thereby becoming the foremost authority on the artist. Another possibility is that the family, his descendants, wishing to secure the recognition of the artist, will donate a substantial body of his work to a museum in a town to which the artist has ties. This usually leads to the organization of an exhibition of the donation, with an accompanying catalogue. Any of these possibilities can occur, and sometimes can even coincide; in any case, they are worthwhile if they ulti-

mately lead to greater knowledge of the artist and save his work from oblivion.

Our subject is Pierre Daura, a Catalan painter who, until 1939, divided his time between Catalonia and France, exhibiting regularly in Barcelona and Paris to the acclaim of a sector of contemporary critics. The fact that he settled in the United States — in rural Virginia to be precise — meant that he lost contact with the European art world and was obliged to adapt to his new American surroundings. Daura slowly disappeared from the Catalan art scene of the gray post-war years, like many other artists of his generation who were forced into exile, mostly in France. But his case was different, for Virginia was far away — geographically and esthetically — from the focus of Paris, where some of them triumphed, or at least managed to maintain links with their native Catalonia.

However, Daura did not leave Europe solely for political reasons. Having fought as a volunteer (at the mature age of forty-one) for the Republicans against the forces of General Franco, once the outcome was clear, he repudiated the new dictatorship imposed on the Spanish state, just as his godfather, Pablo Casals, and so many others did. In his case, there was an added motivation. His wife, Louise Blair, was an American painter whom he met in Paris and married there in 1928. In 1939, Louise became seriously ill with a kidney problem and, accompanied by her family, returned to Virginia for medical treatment. By the time she recovered, World War II had broken out, requiring them to stay in America, as it was impossible for them to return to France. After the mandatory three years of residence, Daura and his daughter, Martha, became naturalized United States citizens.

Daura was a college art teacher in Lynchburg, Virginia, from 1945 to 1953. Teaching not only brought him into contact with young people, but it also allowed him to do experimental work and research which left a mark on his art. In 1953, he gave up teaching, but until 1976, the year of his death, he continued to paint and experiment incessantly, dividing his time between Virginia and St. Cirq Lapopie, a small picturesque village in France above the river Lot, where he had settled with Louise shortly after their marriage and where their daughter, Martha, was born in 1930. I should add that St. Cirq Lapopie was a source of inspiration for his painting throughout his life.

Daura's departure from his homeland and from his chosen place of residence in France — indeed from Europe — virtually isolated him from Paris, which at that time was a creative point of reference for any artist interested in finding out about, and becoming involved in, the most advanced trends in contemporary art. In addition, he had to restart his career in a new country. He was well received, and his work — with the exception of the brief interlude of Cercle et Carré — was basically figurative. Circumstances conspired to give him a name renowned in a few intimate circles, but unknown or fallen by the side of the major routes of contemporary art history. Thus the American Daura became a solitary character, estranged artistically from the Catalan and European colleagues with whom he had shared so many concerns.

The generally accepted critics of the second half of the twentieth century, fascinated by the major contributions of what has been called "avant-garde art", often concentrated their attention on a certain type of work, preventing them from discovering new approaches, depending on the viewpoint of the specific artist. Daura, for example, chose a very different academic path, with figurative roots but very distinctive solutions. Dogmatism is always harmful, because it precludes other possibilities. It was applied to Daura and many other artists of his generation, whether Catalan, European or American, who found themselves in relative geographic isolation and who, as a result, did not belong to one of the major movements of abstraction, abstract expressionism or conceptual art, to mention just some of the main avant-garde trends. It was not until the very end of the twentieth century that these artists, who are in fact very numerous, began to receive their fair share of attention.

In Daura's case, however, there are even more reasons

for his being to some extent forgotten, such as the general disregard of contemporary art museums for artists of his type. These museums take a theoretical approach that tends to exclude any work which does not come strictly under the umbrella of the established — or rather, "official" — avant-garde, however contradictory this may seem.

Furthermore, Daura and his work have been the subject of few bibliographic references of any great import, and he has had a low public profile for the last fifty years, — both while he was still painting and after his death. It is true that Daura did have exhibitions in his adopted country — remember that in 1943, he and his daughter became American citizens — though they were generally in the region of Virginia where he lived and taught. But in Europe, at least in Barcelona, since the exhibition held at the Sala Barcino in 1935, he had not had a solo exhibition. Now, shortly before and at the time of this book's publication — practically the year 2000 — there are a few exhibitions which I will comment on later.

Daura began to receive public attention in 1990, years after his death, when Martha, the only child of Pierre and Louise, organized her father's art and began to make donations of it to various American and European museums; this was the first step in her diligent task of having the artist rediscovered. Martha very judiciously decided to offer works in places with which her father had, at one time or other, a special connection.

A most important initiative undertaken to publicize her father's work was undoubtedly the creation, in 1990, of the Daura Gallery at Lynchburg College, where he had been head of the Art Department during the 1945-1946 academic year. Through gifts in the United States, the artist's work is now in the collections of the Virginia Museum of Fine Arts, in Richmond; the San Antonio Museum of Art, in Texas, which has over twenty paintings and a large collection of drawings; the Chrysler Museum of Art, in Norfolk, Virginia; the St. Petersburg Museum of Fine Arts, in Florida; the Fuller Museum in Brockton, Massachusetts; and the Asheville Museum, in North Carolina.

In Europe, obviously the two countries most closely connected with Daura are Catalonia and France. Martha wanted her father's work to be well represented in both places. Today, in France, his works are in the Centre Georges Pompidou, in Paris; the Musée Paul Dupuy and the Musée des Augustins, in Toulouse; the Musée du Vieux Figeac; the Musée Henri Martin, in Cahors; and, of special significance, the Musée Hyacinthe Rigaud, in Perpignan, which has some fifty paintings. The links between Daura and his family, and this city, are rooted in a deep friendship with Modest Sabaté, the writer and politician who was given refuge by Daura and his wife in St. Cirq in 1936, when Sabaté had to flee Barcelona because of his writing. The Sabaté family later settled in Le Boulou, a small town near the Spanish border, to the southwest of Perpignan.

In Catalonia, after the Daura exhibition at the Sala Barcino in Barcelona in 1935 (organized by Modest Sabaté), and his inclusion in the Saló d'Octubre of 1948, Daura's work was not seen again in public until his daughter undertook to restore his name and place in contemporary art history. In this task, as I mentioned earlier, she was assisted by Teresa Macià, Curator of the Museu de Montserrat — the museum which Martha approached with an offer of her father's work, knowing that this museum had two of his paintings permanently on view — and by Father Josep de C. Laplana, the Director of this museum. The Museu de Montserrat, which has a major collection of nineteenth and twentieth century Catalan art, quickly accepted Martha's gift. Shortly afterwards, in 1995, the museum organized an exhibition with a representative selection of the artist's work. In 1931, Daura had spent a month on the mountain of Montserrat, emblematic of Catalonia, as a participant in the competition organized by the monastery under the title "Montserrat vist pels artistes" (Montserrat as seen by artists). He was awarded the St. Cecilia Prize for one of the two paintings which were on show at the Museu de Montserrat prior to Martha's donation.

The author's role in the rediscovery of the artist goes beyond the context of Montserrat. She was impressed with Daura's work from her first contact with it, and she was the curator of the exhibition of the art given for the Museu Diocesà de Menorca, in Ciutadella, the town where the artist was born, probably prematurely, on the island where he did his compulsory military service from 1917 to 1920. This museum, housed in a newly restored former Augustine monastery, has had a Daura Room since 1996, where a large collection of his paintings are on view. The author also collaborated on a documentary video about the artist, made by Agnès de Sacy, which is available in four languages.

In Catalonia, the Museu d'Art Contemporani de Barcelona has four works from the period of Cercle et Carré, thanks once more to Martha. But the institution which has the largest and most representative collection of Daura's works in our country, also a gift from Martha, is the Museu Nacional d'Art de Catalunya: thirty-four paintings and a very significant group of drawings and engravings. The presence of this collection in the leading art museum of Catalonia, where Daura had not hitherto been represented, represents the "official" rediscovery of the artist in Barcelona. Teresa Macià was responsible for the biographical introduction to the catalogue produced by the museum for the new Daura collection.

Teresa Macià also contributed to other activities related to Daura's work, in addition to the projects and exhibitions already mentioned. Her text in the meticulous catalogue, a foretaste of this book, published by the Barcelona gallery, Sala d'Art Artur Ramon, for an exhibition-sale of the artist's work in February and March, 1999, is ample proof of this.

The author's lively interest in Daura's work led her to study him as a personality from many different angles. She did extensive bibliographical research related to his Catalan and French periods of residence, she met and interviewed people who actually knew him, and she was a frequent guest at the Daura home in St. Cirq. There, assisted by Martha, she was able to study the Daura art kept in the house. She made the most of the opportunity to absorb the St. Cirq landscape which so thrilled Daura during his lifetime. All of this made Teresa Macià an ideal person for the task of converting the idea of a book into reality.

The author spent some time at the Daura Gallery, in Lynchburg, Virginia, where the artist's documentary archives are kept, and visited many places important to his life and work in his adopted country. This allowed her to deepen her research, and to penetrate Daura's American context, so far removed from the European setting of the first stage of his life, and to date completely unknown to European writers. Her knowledge of Daura's St. Cirq world — so carefully illuminated, "revitalized", one might say, by Daura and his wife Louise over the years — makes her a suitable Daura biographer.

In this book, Teresa Macià gives us a general text, containing an introductory overview of Daura's life and art, often based on a large volume of unpublished documents. Her access to this archival material has permitted her to present a new appraisal of Daura. This is a first study of this Franco-Catalan-American artist. We would like, and consider it necessary, to see a comprehensive catalogue raisonné of his extensive, assorted output: painting, drawing, engraving and even sculpture. It is always a vital resource when dealing with a painter of his caliber, and it would assist both professional scholars and art-lovers.

Reading this book, we follow the painter's path from adolescence to his definitive resettlement in Virginia, through that new phase of life on which he then embarked, to his death in Virginia, detached from the European art setting, in an environment so different from the world which had once surrounded him. The man and his deepest thoughts and emotions are revealed to us. From this book, we learn that Daura was always a painter of light, a Mediterranean painter. His beloved St. Cirq landscape became a major leitmotif in his work. Even today, it is still a picturesque little village, like something out of a fairy tale. Daura had a medieval house there which he and his wife restored and turned into their preferred home. But he did not reserve his love solely for the places around St. Cirq, which come to exuberant life in his oils and watercolors from the fifties; Daura was also enamored of the Mediterranean: from Corsica to the coastline of Minorca, the Majorcan coast of Deya, of Altafulla... And, as much, of the trees of Virginia and the Allegheny Mountains, so far from his native land.

Daura's work exudes a Mediterranean air. He always had affection for, and very close ties with, the Mediterranean world, both Catalan and French. There was an ever-present nostalgia, a yearning for his old-world roots: Virginia was both distant and different. His horror of war — the Spanish Civil War and all its consequences, World War I and World War II — left a mark. There was a poignant feeling which never left him, and which often manifested itself in his work, in his strong, expressive engravings, and in his paintings and drawings. His paintings include an extensive

group of self-portraits which, viewed together, give perhaps the best account of his inner feelings, of aging.

Daura's place in art history to date has been based primarily on his participation in the group Cercle et Carré, and on his collaboration with Torres-García. In reality, the relationship between the two was much that of equals, and more than once it was Torres-García who found himself in debt to Daura. For example, it was Daura who organized the Torres-García exhibition at the Galerie A. G. Fabre, in Paris in June 1926. The proceeds from this exhibition allowed the Catalan-Uruguayan painter and his family to move to Paris from Villefranche-sur-Mer, where they had been living. In 1928, the Salon d'Automne in Paris refused works by both painters (who had kept in close contact since 1926) along with works by their colleagues, — Jean Hélion, Alfred Aberdam and Engel-Rozier, — prompting the five artists to organize a parallel exhibition. The concerns of the two painters were similar, and this exhibition was another step in forming the relationship which was to bring them together artistically the following year.

After his marriage to Louise Blair, the Dauras moved to the rue Marcel Sembat in Paris, where they lived in the same apartment complex as the Torres-García family. This was when Torres-García, Michel Seuphor and Daura developed the idea of what was to become Cercle et Carré — that is, the creation of a group whose art was based on abstract, constructivist, and geometric principles, as opposed to dreamlike, subconscious surrealism, which was then so much in vogue, but so removed from their beliefs. The group's name, Cercle et Carré (Circle and Square), was Seuphor's idea, but it was Daura who produced its graphic emblem, which was reproduced on its printed matter. The group's first and only exhibition was held in April 1930, in Paris, and only three issues of its review were published. Daura's artistic experimentation did not end here, although henceforth he worked individually, and not as a member of any ideological group. As a result, his public profile was very different, but his work continued to be just as interesting.

All of this, and much more, such as Daura's friendship with the poet, André Breton, in the early fifties, and his family association with another painter, Jean Hélion, who married Jean Blair, Louise's sister, are shown. Teresa Macià introduces us to this remarkable artist, and underscores the value of his work, to give him the place he deserves in the history of Catalan and world art.

Following her text, there is an epilogue by Francesc Fontbona, one of the great authorities on nineteenth and twentieth century Catalan art, who places Daura in the Catalan artistic context prior to the Spanish Civil War, as a member of what he refers to as "the generation of 1917". This monograph is a crucial point of reference for the rediscovery and subsequent study of the artist.

These few lines, rather than a conventional foreword, are intended to be, as the title suggests, a prologue to a rediscovery, to the rediscovery of Pierre Daura.

# Pierre Daura

## ( 1896 - 1976 )

TERESA MACIÀ

# FOREWORD

Two paintings by Pierre Daura have been exhibited at the Museum of Montserrat, among the great masters of the so-called Catalan School, ever since the Modern Painting Section was opened in 1982 with the extraordinary collection given to the Monastery by Josep Sala i Ardiz. The Daura works chosen by the Museum's director, Father Josep de C. Laplana, were the painting which won the 1931 St. Cecilia prize in the competition Montserrat Seen by Artists, and the 1934 Virginia landscape donated to the Museum by Josep Maria Calvó i Vilardebó.

The quality of the works was undeniable. Yet the artist was almost unknown to the public. Those two paintings and the short biographies in the *Diccionari Biogràfic Ràfols d'Artistes Catalans* and the *Enciclopèdia Catalana* were not much for a painter who, in 1919, had been a founding member of the Agrupació d'Artistes Catalans (Group of Catalan Artists), and who had received very favorable critiques on exhibitions in Barcelona and Paris in the twenties and thirties. In 1937, Joan Merli included Daura in the book *33 Pintors Catalans* (33 Catalan Painters) and ended his short biography with the following words: "Let us hope that our generation will make due amends to one of our best independent creators."

In 1995, I met the artist's daughter, Martha Daura, when she came to Montserrat to donate thirty oils and one sculpture by her father. Martha revealed to me some aspects of her father's life that I found fascinating: a painter who was at the forefront of the artistic avant-garde in Barcelona and Paris, who chose to fight in a civil war when freedom and democracy were threatened and who, to keep faith with his principles, went into exile far from the centers of his former artistic activity and followed a solitary creative path.

Daura's life, which Martha described to me, became even more meaningful when I visited St. Cirq Lapopie, France, and saw much of his art: landscapes, still lifes and figure studies of superb technique and extraordinary color. Martha told me that she had preserved her father's correspondence, notebooks and diaries. Each time we met, she disclosed more details of Daura's life, revealing an increasingly admirable person. In 1996, I was the curator of the permanent exhibition of the Daura art which Martha gave to the Diocesan Museum of Minorca in Ciutadella, and a year later I began the biography which is the principal part of this book.

The extensive archives illustrate the human side of this great painter: a cultivated, sensitive and socially committed man. An artist who lived to create and who strove to mirror in his work the concerns of twentieth-century man. Daura's art and life — two inseparable facets of a single existence — make us reflect on the meaning of war and the role which art plays in society, and make us think more deeply about our recent history.

Martha Daura has undertaken to have her father rediscovered. Her gifts of his art to Catalan, French and American museums, the documentary video illustrating his life and art, and this book are examples of her efforts to rescue the reputation of her father from the anonymity in which it was shrouded because of his voluntary isolation from the centers of twentieth-century artistic life.

I could not have written this book without the help of many people whom I now wish to thank. First and foremost, I would like to express my gratitude to: Martha Daura and Thomas Mapp; the Daura family in Barcelona; Pilar Vélez and Francesc Fontbona, co-authors of this book; Father Josep de C. Laplana, Director of the Museu de Montserrat; Eduard Carbonell and Cecília Vidal, Director and Curator of Engravings and Drawings of the Museu Nacional d'Art de Catalunya in Barcelona. I also wish to thank everyone involved at the following institutions: Daura Gallery of Lynchburg College, Virginia; Museu Nacional d'Art de Catalunya, Museu d'Art Contemporani and Sala d'Art Artur Ramon, Barcelona; Museu Diocesà de Menorca, Ciutadella; Musée Hyacinthe Rigaud, Perpignan; Musée des Augustins and Musée Paul Dupuy, Toulouse; Centre Pompidou, Paris; Musée du Vieux Figeac, Figeac; San Antonio Museum of Art, Texas; St. Petersburg's Museum of Fine Arts, Florida; Museum of Fine Arts, Richmond, and Chrysler Museum of Art, Norfolk, Virginia.

**Joan Daura Sendra.** 1930.
Etching, 28 x 21.8 cm.
MNAC, Barcelona. Photograph: Calveras, Mérida, Sagristà.

# CHILDHOOD AND EDUCATION: BARCELONA

**Pierre Daura, age 4.** ca. 1900.
Daura Archives.

Pierre Daura was born on the island of Minorca in February 1896. He probably arrived early, taking his parents by surprise while they were traveling, and it was not until they returned to their home in Barcelona that they registered his birth: Pedro Francisco Juan Daura y García, born February 21, 1896. In Catalonia, his home region of Spain, he is known as Pere. When he went to Paris in 1914, he was required to use the French equivalent, Pierre, on his identity papers, and from that time on, he has been known as Pierre everywhere except in Catalonia.

Pierre's father, Joan Daura i Sendra, had a textile printing factory in Les Corts, Sarrià, a suburb of Barcelona. The textile business supported the family, but Joan's true vocation was music. For years he was able to combine the two activities, and he was a percussionist in the orchestra of the opera house, the Gran Teatre del Liceu in Barcelona.

Pierre was the first child of Joan and Rosa García i Martínez. Her death in January 1904 left Joan Daura alone with three children: Pierre, who was not yet eight, and his younger brother and sister, Ricard and Mercè.

As a young boy, Pierre began to show an interest in art, but his father did his best to make the boy change his mind. Pierre's chance meetings with a painter on several occasions after school had their effect on the boy's decision to paint. At the age of seventy, he still vividly recalled the hours he spent admiring the "magic" that the painter created with his pencils and brushstrokes of color.[1]

Joan Daura finally gave in to Pierre's insistence, and allowed his son to devote himself to art. Pierre studied at La Llotja (School of Fine Arts) and attended some night classes at the Ateneu Enciclopèdic Popular and the Acadèmia Gelabert. The moment came when the textile business profits were no longer enough, and Pierre, the eldest of the children, had to bring money into the household. Through Joan Daura's contacts in the theater world, he found his son a job with the theater set designer, Joaquim Jiménez i Solà.[2] Pierre had to find time for both his studies and his work. Daura had various teachers in his classes at La Llotja, but he

**Pierre Daura, age 14.** ca. 1910.
Daura Archives.

**Estudi Vert.** Barcelona. 1910-13.
Watercolor on paper, 53.2 x 48.2 cm.
MNAC, Barcelona. Photograph: Calveras, Mérida, Sagristà.

**Ex Libris Estudi Vert.** 1915.
Mixed media on paper, 28.3 x 18.7 cm.
MNAC, Barcelona. Photograph: Calveras, Mérida, Sagristà.

remembered two above all: José Ruiz Blasco, Pablo Picasso's father, and Josep Calvo i Verdonces, who encouraged him to go to Paris.

It was probably in late 1910 or early 1911 that Daura and two fellow students, Agapit Vidal Salichs (1894-1962) and Emili Bosch-Roger (1894-1980), rented a small room near the Plaça de Santa Caterina, which they christened "Estudi Vert" (Green Studio). There they painted and showed their work publicly for the first time, in November 1911.[3] Daura sold his first painting, a Cézannesque landscape, to the

painter Emili Pascual Monturiol. The following year, they repeated the experience in a small rented room in a medieval house at 42, Carrer dels Mercaders, which still exists in the heart of Barcelona's old quarter.[4] In addition to Cézannesque, greenish-ochre landscapes, Daura painted the port with its boats and piers: nebulous, dark-toned views with reflections of light on the water, done with short strokes of bright color. The cathedral and the streets around his studio were other subjects he often painted in oils, and drew in charcoal.

1. Daura memoirs, Tape 5, Daura Archives.

2. A business card of Jiménez Solà's set designing firm is in the Daura Archives.

3. *La Publicitat*, Barcelona, November 23, 1911. The address of the first studio was Plaça de Santa Caterina, 1, 4th floor, and it was open to the public from

November 12 to December 20, 1911. The invitation cards are in the Daura Archives.

4. The show was from November 24 to December 1, 1912. The invitations cards are in the Daura Archives.

**Monastery of Pedralbes**, 1913.
Gouache on paper, 51.2 x 69.5 cm.
MNAC, Barcelona. Photograph: Calveras, Mérida, Sagristà.

**Boats in Harbor.** ca. 1908.
Oil on cardboard, 30 x 39 cm.
Martha Daura collection, 2005.  Photograph: Paige Critcher.

**Harbor Reflections.** ca. 1908.
Oil on cardboard, 35 x 42 cm.
Musée Hyacinthe Rigaud. Perpignan. Photograph: Michel Jauze.

**Barcelona Harbor.** ca. 1914.
Oil on cardboard, 50 x 64 cm.
Museu Diocesà de Menorca. Ciutadella. Photograph: Cisco Moll.

**Port of Barcelona.** ca. 1911.
Mixed media on paper, 57 x 48 cm.
MNAC, Barcelona. Photograph: Calveras, Mérida, Sagristà..

**Medieval Quarter.** Barcelona. ca. 1911.
Mixed media on paper, 58.8 x 48.5 cm.
MNAC, Barcelona. Photograph: Calveras, Mérida, Sagristà.

**Port of Barcelona.** ca. 1914.
Oil on canvas, 29 x 35 cm.
Martha Daura collection, 2384. Photograph: Paige Critcher.

**Barge.** Barcelona. 1910-14.
Oil on canvas, 29 x 34 cm.
Martha Daura collection, 2408. Photograph: Paige Critcher.

**Self-portrait.** ca. 1920.
Gouache on paper, 38 x 27 cm. Private collection. Photograph: Martí Gasull.

# THE YOUNG ARTIST: PARIS

In early 1914, Daura was earning less money because of a decline in the business of the Jiménez Solà workshop. He had an excuse to leave home. His godfather, the cellist Pablo Casals, convinced his father that all aspiring artists should spend time in Paris. Daura fulfilled his dream of going to the French capital to complete his art education. He arrived in the spring of 1914 with letters of introduction from Casals and Calvo, his teacher at La Llotja.

In Paris Daura first worked as an apprentice in the studio of Émile Bernard, where he catalogued the letters from Van Gogh. He also studied engraving with André Lambert, the editor of the Latin review *Janus*, and learned woodcut engraving from his fellow Catalan, Lluís Jou.

Unfortunately, the outbreak of World War I interrupted Daura's enjoyment of Paris. He did not want to return to Barcelona, and he tried to enlist in the French army, but as a minor he was unable to do so without parental permission. As the war drew on, foreigners were asked to help in the defense effort, and Daura was assigned to a Renault munitions factory. The days he spent alone in Paris had a marked effect on him. Much later, he was to recall days when everything seemed to be painted in black, as though the city had been abandoned,[5] and his art of the Paris period reflected this.

During these years in Paris, Daura frequently saw fellow Catalan artists Lluís Bracons and his wife Enriqueta Pascual Benigani, Manuel Cano, Joan Sandalinas, Francesc Vidal Gomà, Jacint Salvadó, Gustavo Cochet and Pere Créixams.[6]

From 1917 to 1920 Daura did his compulsory military service on Minorca. Billeted with his cavalry unit in the barracks of Villa Carlos (Es Castell) on the outskirts of Mahon, Daura spent his free time drawing the Minorcan landscape. He was responsible for provisions, which freed him to move around the island, and to capture many of its coves and ports in his drawings. While he was in Minorca, he kept up an interesting correspondence with Émile Bernard, who sent him advice on how to direct his artistic career: "Do not let the idea of perfection in your art stop you. Simply go straight

**Daura in Uniform.** ca. 1918.
Daura Archives.

ahead, brush in hand. Your gifts, nature studied and seen in its entirety, your dreams of art will do the rest. I advise you not to enslave yourself to any school. Seek Beauty. That is what one does not seek enough. It surrounds us, however, in

**View of Paris.** 1917.
Pencil on paper, 35.2 x 40 cm.
MNAC, Barcelona. Photograph: Calveras, Mérida, Sagristà.

the simplest things that God has made. (I do not say that man has made.) Genius, which is the reflection of God, is our only consolation for all the abominations of so-called progress....."[7]

While on Minorca, Daura kept in touch with his painter friends in Barcelona, with whom he founded the Agrupació d'Artistes Catalans (Group of Catalan Artists) in 1919.[8] The group's first exhibition, in February 1919 at the Galeries Dalmau, presented works by Emili Bosch-Roger, Daura, Pere Farró, Josep Girbau, Ferran Musons, Miquel Muntané, Josep Salvà, Agapit Vidal Salichs, Francesc Vidal Gomà and Jaume Vila. Daura showed four drawings. The foreword to the exhibition catalogue outlined the intentions of this group of artists: "We follow no set path — we will go where the trends of the time lead us, and as far ahead as we can go."[9] This was almost a premonition of the path that Daura was to tread. Later the group was joined by Aurora Fontecha, Héctor Ragni, Ferran Callicó, Pere Jou, Pere Dalmau, Lluís Bracons, Manuel Cano, Pere Créixams and Gustavo Cochet. The last four artists also lived in Paris, and were close friends of Daura.

When Daura completed his military service, he returned to Paris. Until 1925, he moved around a great deal. He was in Montmartre and then Montparnasse — in La Ruche —[10] but always in poor districts, where other artists with limited means lived.

In December 1920 and January 1921, he accompanied an American painter, Charles Logasa,[11] on a trip around Spain,

which included Toledo, Aranjuez, Madrid, El Escorial, Segovia, Valladolid and Burgos. Some of the landscapes he drew on that journey were exhibited in Barcelona in 1922, at the Galeria Dalmau in a show of the Group of Catalan Artists.[12] He took part in the Salon d'Automne in Paris in the autumn of 1922.[13]

Daura traveled extensively in France and Belgium, and his landscapes focus on the streets, ports and beaches he saw: Biarritz, Bailleul and Lille (1922), Cherbourg (1923), Angervilliers, Beauvais and Chartres (1924), Collioure and Cassis (1925), Bruges and Ostende (1926), Cassis and Vers (1927). While landscape was his favorite subject when he traveled, when he worked in his studio it was still life and figure study. Some of the landscapes and still lifes of this period suggest the influence of Cézanne, Émile Bernard and Amedeo Modigliani.

In May 1923, while Daura was working for the firm Gaetan Jeanin Ingr. of Billancourt on a mural for a hotel in Cherbourg, Normandy, the scaffolding collapsed. The injuries he sustained in the fall were serious enough to keep

**Still life.** 1917.
Pencil on paper, 32 x 24 cm.
MNAC, Barcelona. Photograph: Calveras, Mérida, Sagristà.

him hospitalized for several months in Cherbourg, and as a result of the accident, he had a permanently clenched left hand.

During the early twenties in Paris, Daura was a frequent companion of the Catalan painter, Pere Créixams, who lived in Montmartre (many years later he recalled the time when the resident artists declared Montmartre an independent Republic). With Créixams and a mutual friend, the writer and poet Marcel Sauvage, Daura took part in a street fair in which he sold all of his drawings to the dealer D. H. Kahnweiler.[14]

In 1925, with Gustavo Cochet, an Argentine-Catalan painter whom Daura had met in Barcelona, he went into the business of designing and making silk batiks. The operation went quite well, but only for a short time, as the workshop was destroyed by fire in 1926. Later Cochet opened a successor workshop and continued in the batik design business in association with another Catalan, Senabre.

In 1927, Daura participated in Barcelona in a show with the Group of Catalan Artists,[15] and in Paris at the Galerie La Sélection, in an exhibition of modern painting which brought together twenty-nine artists. The aim of Marcel Sauvage, who organized the latter show, was to hold a series of exhibitions which would illustrate the various trends of contemporary art.[16] Daura was given a contract with La Sélection, to paint seascapes, which lasted over a year. During this period, he also did a group of engravings of Paris cityscapes and of Minorcan landscapes. He excelled in this technique because of the purity of his lines.

In late 1927, Daura met Louise Blair (1905-1972), an American who had recently graduated from Bryn Mawr College, and they became engaged in February 1928. On December 20, after overcoming the opposition of Louise's family, the couple married. Louise was not the only member of the Blair family to settle in Europe. At the Daura wedding, one of the bride's sisters, Jean Blair, met the painter Jean Hélion, whom she married in September 1932.

During the period of their engagement in 1928, Daura and Louise spent some months painting on the island of Corsica. They were chaperoned by Louise's cousin, Anne Matthews. The rural life of the island interior, the coves, bays and ports of the coast, the churches and the narrow streets merging into the horizon or out to sea, these were the subjects which dominated his works, which were admired in Paris (Galerie René Zivy, December 1-28, 1928)[17] and in Barcelona (Sala Badrinas, May 18-June 9, 1929).[18]

5. Daura memoirs, Tape 1, Daura Archives.

6. Drawings and engravings by these artist friends were donated by the artist's daughter, Martha Daura, to the Museu Nacional d'Art de Catalunya (MNAC), Barcelona.

7. "*Que l'idée de la perfection de votre art ne vous arrête pas. Allez tout simplement devant vous, le pinceau à la main. Vos dons, la nature etudiée et vue par sa generalité, vos rêves d'art feront le reste. Ce que je vous conseille c'est de ne vous inféoder a aucune école. Cherchez le Beau. C'est qu'on ne cherche pas assez. Il nous entoure pourtant dans les plus simples choses que Dieu a faites. (Je ne dis pas que l'homme a faites.) Le Genie qui est le reflet de Dieu, nous console seul de toutes les abominations d'un pretendu progrès....*" Letter from Émile Bernard to Daura, undated, Daura Archives.

8. Francesc Fontbona: *El paisatgisme a Catalunya*, Destino, Barcelona, 1979, pp. 273, 294, 296-98; Francesc Miralles: "L'època de les avantguardes 1917-1970", *Història de l'art català*, Vol. VIII, Edicions 62, Barcelona, 1983, p. 30.

9. *Agrupació d'Artistes Catalans*, I Exhibition, Galeries Dalmau, Barcelona, February 1-15, 1919.

10. For the life of the artists who lived in the complex called La Ruche, built in late 1900 by the sculptor Alfred Boucher, see Jeanine Warnod: *La Ruche &*

*Montparnasse*, Weber, Geneva-Paris, 1978; and René Barotte: *La Ruche d'Hier et d'Aujourd'hui*, Galerie de Berri, Paris, February 12-March 5, 1949.

11. Charles Logasa (1883-1935) was introduced to the Catalan group in Paris by Torres-García; see Joaquín Torres-García: *Historia de mi vida*, Paidós, Barcelona - Buenos Aires - Mexico, 1990, p. 184. (1st edition, Montevideo, 1939)

12. *Catalunya Gràfica*, Barcelona, No 5, February 20, 1922.

13. *19ème Salon d'Automne*, Catalogue, Paris, 1922.

14. The drawings brought 350 FF, an extraordinary sum of money for Daura at that time. Daura memoirs, Tape 4, Daura Archives.

15. *Agrupació d'Artistes Catalans*, IV Exhibition, Galeries Dalmau, Barcelona, 1925. In 1927, Daura exhibited with the same group at the Sala Parés, Barcelona.

16. *Peinture Moderne*, Catalogue, La Sélection, Paris, 1927.

17. *Pierre Daura*, Galerie René Zivy, Paris, 1928.

18. Màrius Gifreda: "Pere Daura", *Mirador*, Barcelona, No. 18, May 30, 1929, p. 7; and R. V.: "Paisatges de Corsega", *El Matí*, Barcelona, May 31, 1929; and "Exposicions", *La Vanguardia*, Barcelona, June 12, 1929.

Ep. d'artiste

Calafons a Minorque

**Calafons a Minorque.** 1927.
Etching, 13 x 17.8 cm.
MNAC, Barcelona. Photograph: Calveras, Mérida, Sagristà.

11/20                                          *ours*

*Rue Clovis. Paris Vᵉ.*                 *Coll. L. B. de*

**Rue Clovis.** Paris. ca. 1924.
Etching, 25.6 x 31.7 cm.
MNAC, Barcelona. Photograph: Calveras, Mérida, Sagristà

**View of Paris.** 1914-17.
Oil on canvas, 40 x 48 cm.
Private collection. Photograph: Martí Gasull.

**Villa Carlos.** Minorque. ca. 1927.
Etching, 21 x 24.5 cm.
MNAC, Barcelona. Photograph: Calveras, Mérida, Sagristà.

**Sailboat at Collioure.** ca. 1925.
Oil on canvas, 54 x 65 cm.
Museu Diocesà de Menorca, Ciutadella. Photograph: Cisco Moll.

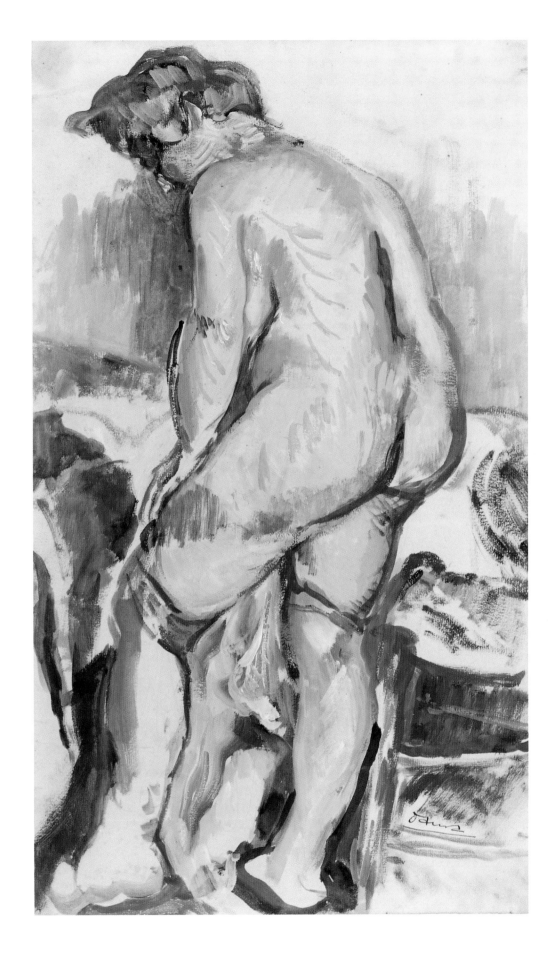

**Nude.** ca. 1925.
Gouache on paper, 48 x 28 cm. Private collection. Photograph: Martí Gasull.

**Louise in Red Beret.** ca. 1927.
Oil on canvas, 79 x 64 cm.
Virginia Museum of Fine Arts, Richmond. Photograph: Katherine Wetzel.

# BETWEEN REPRESENTATION AND ABSTRACTION

**Daura and his wife Louise.** 1939.
Photograph: Howard Hammerley. Daura Archives.

In 1925, Charles Logasa asked Daura to find a gallery in Paris which would exhibit the work of the Uruguayan-Catalan painter, Joaquín Torres-García. After some time in New York and Italy, Torres-García had settled near his friend Logasa in Villefranche-sur-Mer, a little village on the Provençal coast, near Nice. Daura made the rounds of the Paris galleries,[19] and asked for help from his friend Pau Gargallo, one of the artists "who has already made a name for himself".[20] Daura wanted to ask Picasso for help, but when Torres-García complained of the disagreeableness of Picasso the last time Torres-García had visited him, Daura gave up the idea.[21] In Barcelona, where Daura spent a few weeks because of his father's illness, he went to see Josep Dalmau, who organized a Torres-García exhibition at his gallery.[22]

Torres-García urged Daura to come to Villefranche-sur-Mer to see his work: "as you know the Paris art market, you will be able to make a more judicious choice."[23] Torres-García was developing different styles, and he was not at all sure which would suit the tastes of the French market at the time. Daura went to Villefranche-sur-Mer in May 1926 to see Torres-García. But he made the most of this trip; he did a series of drawings, and he visited the writer and Republican politician, Vicent Blasco Ibáñez (1867-1928), who had been living near Nice (in Menton) since the coup of Primo de Rivera in 1923. Blasco Ibáñez advised Torres-García to leave the Côte d'Azur, and to settle in Paris.[24]

When he returned to Paris, Daura managed to organize an exhibition for Torres-García at the Galerie Fabre. He selected and framed the paintings, restoring some of them, and organized the publicity.[25] After the exhibition opened, Torres-García became ill and returned home to Villefranche-sur-Mer. Daura then stayed at the gallery to meet the customers and to promote his friend's work. Daura's health suffered from the pressure of the efforts to help Torres-García, and it was another Catalan friend, the doctor Francesc Duran i Reynals, who provided Daura with medicine and urged him to leave Paris for a few weeks' rest.

Proceeds from the Galerie Fabre sale made it possible for Torres-García to move to Paris with his family. They first lived in a studio lent to them by Jean Hélion (Jean Bichier),[26] and then in an apartment complex at rue Marcel Sembat where other artists lived, and where the Dauras were also to move.

The friendship with Torres-García produced a major change in Daura's painting, and some of Torres-García's lengthy reflections on art are included in the correspondence between the two artists. In June 1927, Torres-García, after criticizing cubism for being a mute, inhuman form of painting, wrote: "I believe that all painters have to practice a kind of gymnastics like cubism, that is to say not copy the real, keep only the essential, and then represent nature very freely, like a true miracle-worker, in other words, create. But they [the cubists and Picasso's followers] think that for it to be genuine creation it should not resemble anything, and this is where the mistake lies. This is where their lack of humanity and poetry lies.... In their search for painting, the others have lost their human vision of painting. The right direction...."[27] "Those of us who abstract something essential

**Daura** with friends after the opening of the first Torres-García Paris exhibition, June 1926. Left to right: Martí, Ramon Jou Senabre, Duran Reynals, Balcells, Daura, Torres-García, Puig and Ramon Sastre. Daura Archives.

from reality build a world and objects in our own style. That is true creation. Sensitivity and emotion are channeled through intelligence. We are artists, architects, if you will. The others can only do something when in front of an object, they copy its real appearance and are slaves to all they have before them. They are unable to create an image. Now, I believe that they have to make this leap and put themselves on our plane. But not everyone is able to do just that.... I believe, dear Daura, that you are gifted enough to make that leap and launch yourself onto this plane of ours...."[28]

Daura explained to Torres-García that, during the months he spent painting on Corsica, he was so drawn to the natural beauty of his surroundings that he could not help painting it. Torres-García answered in the following words: "You tell me that you have not been able to escape the influence of nature's beauty. Do not be concerned. It is better that way. Do not worry. I happen to think that this is better for you than anything else.... Now, more than ever, I repeat my old advice to you: create, with color and geometry, something beyond reality. We do not seek the artistic meaning in reality, but within ourselves — just as a musician does with sounds. Painting has to move in an ideal, free environment and create its own light — and we must respect the surface

of the painting — not the 4th dimension, in all its breadth and height, and that's it. Purged of all sensation, pure."[29] It was during the stay on Corsica that Daura painted some of his most remarkable landscapes. The ports, the streets and the sea are transferred to the canvas with fast, vibrant brushstrokes, which some critics have compared to those of Van Gogh.[30] The use of color is lively and original.

In 1928, the jury of the Salon d'Automne rejected a work submitted by Daura, as well as those submitted by Torres-García, Engel-Rozier, Hélion and Aberdam. The five artists joined forces and exhibited their rejected works at the Galerie Marck. Their show of protest received wide and favorable coverage in the press. With their innovative work, they intended to challenge the retrograde movement which, in their opinion, was holding back French art.[31] Daura's rejected work was a still life with fruit scattered across a table, a well structured work with overtones of Cézanne, in which a piece of paper, a bag and a melon support a lyrical display of color.

In addition to his art and his correspondence with many artists, Daura left a personal diary. Unfortunately, it covers only a brief period. In August 1928, Daura wrote: "Worked all day until 6 p.m. Badly. Worse. Will I ever be able to bring out what is deep in my subconscious? To construct a painting. To avoid nature. Above all to have something to say. I think the biggest obstacles to putting my idea and its execution in direct and exact accord are first the technique I learned. Then to have looked too long at nature, to have recreated too much what I have seen only as a technician, rather than as an esthetician. Too much a journeyman painter! When an object was the subject of my observation, I did not think of the canvas and its esthetic meaning. And of a pictorial whole. Misery kept me from painting, so I painted mechanically. Brushstroke by brushstroke. That is my tragic mistake."[32]

In letters to her family in America, Louise described the different artistic movements which coexisted in Paris in the late twenties: "*At present at Paris there are three tendencies, that of the reactionaries, headed by Camille Mauclair, the old critic, who writes philippics against all foreign artists, and upholds any and all French artists who aren't 'Cubist', 'Fauve', or 'Sur-realist'. Then there is the Sur-Realist group, which is sweeping all before it, and is the white hope of all the merchants. The third is the Elementarists, or Constructivists, or Neo-Plasticists, all that believe in abstract art that is 'constructed' no matter how it manifests itself. … Fauvism is now a thing of the past.*"[33]

Daura was immersed in the avant-garde artistic philosophy. He shared its anxious search for truth and perfection in art, which moved him towards the abstract constructivists.

In July 1929, the Dauras moved from rue Pierre Larousse to rue Marcel Sembat, where they occupied a sixth-floor studio which had been Jean Hélion's, in the same apartment block in which Torres-García and the sculptor Joseph Csaky lived.[34] The friendship between the Daura and Torres-García families became even closer from then on, and portraits of the Torres-García children were engraved by Daura and painted by Louise.[35] Daura became acquainted with the art critic, Joseph Milbauer; the painter Camille Descossy; John Xceron, a naturalized American-Greek painter; Benjamino Bufano, a sculptor born in Rome; Michel Seuphor, a French writer and painter of Belgian extraction; and the Dutch members of the De Stijl group such as Piet Mondrian and Theo van Doesburg.

From autumn 1928 through 1929, Daura's work moved increasingly towards abstraction. Always starting from nature, whether from a still life or a landscape, he produced a bold, well structured formal synthesis with a sober range of colors, seldom totally masking the initial figurative reference. Daura's evolution was similar to that of Torres-García.[36] Other Catalan figurative painters went through a non-figurative period during these years, such as Josep de Togores, who between 1928 and 1930 utilized a completely new style, close to surrealist automatism.[37]

Daura and Louise visited Catalonia during the spring of 1929. They painted in the countryside around Tarragona, and stayed several weeks in Altafulla where a friend, Carles Albesa, had asked Daura to design a fresco on the life of Saint Francis. Louise posed as a model for various figures significant in the saint's life. Daura also worked on the design of a fresco on the life of Saint Bonaventure for the private chapel of Bonaventura Barba, in Tarragona.[38]

Some of Daura's landscapes of Tarragona, and of Corsica done the previous year, were exhibited at the Sala Badrinas in Barcelona. Torres-García wrote a critical introduction to Daura's exhibition, praising his "gift for painting", and at the same time anticipating that changes would occur in his work "when he moves from his current naturalist focus to less objective forms".[39]

Landscapes of Ascó, where the Daura family originated, of Altafulla and La Fatarella, painted in Catalonia during that spring of 1929, served the artist as a model for a series of

**Daura preliminary designs for Cercle et Carré logo.** 1929.
Daura Archives.

**Logo of group Cercle et Carré.**
Daura design on heading of group review.

engravings. These were meticulously worked, stylistically *noucentista* (classic modern), and similar to work being produced at the time by Joaquim Sunyer and Joan Colom. Some of these landscapes were used by Daura as figurative references for subsequent constructivist abstract works. One specific example is a representative landscape of Altafulla now at the Museu de Montserrat, which was the model for a near abstract painting now at the Museu d'Art Contemporani de Barcelona.

In the autumn of 1929, Daura offered to translate an article about new Catalan architecture, from Catalan into French or English, for van Doesburg.[40] Daura's circle of acquaintances expanded as he met Luis Fernández, Amédée Ozenfant, Otto van Rees, Hans Arp and Luigi Russolo. Albert Junyent[41] and Joan Junyer were Catalan painters whom Daura saw frequently in Paris. In 1930, he met Georges Vantongerloo while he and Louise were visiting Mondrian at his home.[42]

In November 1929, Daura participated in a show at the Galeria Dalmau, in Barcelona: Arte Moderno Nacional y Extranjero (National and Foreign Modern Art). Works of Daura and Louise Blair were shown beside those of their friends: Pere Créixams, Gustavo Cochet, Joan Junyer, Joan Sandalinas, Josep M. de Sucre, Joaquín Torres-García, Luis Fernández, Jean Hélion, Piet Mondrian, Theo van Doesburg, Georges Vantongerloo, Otto van Rees and John Xceron. In his text for the exhibition catalogue, Magí Cassanyes described the artists brought together as "those who have totally abandoned external appearance in favor of internal representation".[43]

The artistic environment in which Daura lived during this period drew him to abstraction. Torres-García and van Does-

burg praised his abstract work and insisted that he exhibit with them in Holland.[44] The formal synthesis reflected in Daura's abstract art maintained the rich, lively color range which had characterized his earlier work.[45] Only rarely did he choose pure abstraction; he usually left a figurative reference visible in his work.

Louise's letters to her family are a vital source of information about Daura's art; they often give us the reasons for a change in style: *"Pierre's new painting is none of the 'freak' sort. It is a sort of rationalization and geometrising of painting. The Constructivists think that a painting should be pure, i.e… pure color, and pure form, and that having any subject matter takes away from the purity, as one thinks more about the subject than the actual quality of the painting…. Therefore they abolish the subject matter and occupy themselves with volumes of color and the perfect equilibre and construction of the picture…. It is distinctly sober, and for me is not 'complete', as I think that an artist ought to be something more than a geometrician. But at least it is a serious and sober step against all the lawlessness and bad painting that parades and struts under the name of modern Art."*[46]

In the autumn of 1929, Torres-García, Seuphor and Daura decided to form a group. They were motivated by a desire to mobilize artists interested in promoting geometric construction and abstraction, in opposition to the irrational spontaneity of surrealism. On November 24, Daura wrote in his diary: "At 4 p.m. went with the Torres-Garcías to Seuphor's. Received very cordially. We tried to define the possible creation of a group of all those who work in constructivism. Mondrian at the head…."[47] Drafting the group's declaration of intention led to long discussions; some thought that it was not enough simply to oppose surrealism, but that they should come out positively in favor of something else.[48] Deciding which artists should be asked to join the group was also grounds for controversy. The likes and dislikes among the various members were resolved by the creation of two sections, one headed by Torres-García and the other by van Doesburg. Daura recorded the events in his diary: "In order to avoid disagreeable relations, we thought it necessary to divide the group in two sections, A and B. Torres' antipathy to Engel, Hélion and Wants made it necessary."[49]

The group was initially called "Construction",[50] until Seuphor came up with the idea of calling it Cercle et Carré (Circle and Square). He considered that these two geometric forms were the simplest representation of the totality of things; the rational and the sensorial worlds, the earth and the sky of ancient Chinese symbolism, the geometry of straight and of curved lines, male and female.[51] But obtaining agreement was another matter, for the majority initially rejected Seuphor's suggestion. However, Seuphor stood by his proposal and asked Daura, via Torres-García, to design a logo based on a circle and square: "Would you ask Daura to design our emblem (the name of the magazine) on a paper of this size. He is used to that, I think. It should be done as quickly as possible.... I would like, however, to ask your advice as well as Daura's on everything. At 3 we are more intelligent than alone.... I will come to your place and (or) Daura's Wednesday the 25th at 3 p.m. to pick up Daura's drawing...."[52] Daura's design combining the circle and square so pleased everyone that it ended the debate; Cercle et Carré was accepted as the group's name. Daura's experience with design, mentioned by Seuphor, is probably a reference to the cover he had just designed for the Italian edition of John Reed's book, *Ten Days That Shook the World*.[53]

Cercle et Carré's first and only exhibition was held from April 18 to May 1, 1930, at Galerie 23, in Paris. It included works of other artists who sympathized with the group, in addition to those of group members. Daura presented two works, entitled *Ordre* and *Elan discipliné*, and designed the exhibition poster. Like the exhibition of the "Cinq Refusés", the Cercle et Carré exhibition brought an international group of artists together: Francisca Clausen (Denmark), Jean Arp, J. Gorin and Marcelle Cahn (France), Joaquín Torres-García (Uruguay), Piet Mondrian (Holland), Pierre Daura (Spain), Michel Seuphor and Georges Vantongerloo (Belgium), Vordemberge-Gildewart and Kurt Schwitters (Germany), Vera Idelson, Anton Pevsner and W. Kandinsky (Russia), and Luigi Russolo (Italy). The inclusion of artists of various nationalities who were working along similar lines was, for them, confirmation that their common artistic language was current; the international composition of the group verified the modernity of their art.

The difficulty in reaching a consensus among the various members of the group, however, went deeper than disagreements concerning their declaration of intentions, or decision as to who should form part of the group, and selection of a group name and emblem. The differences in the personalities of certain members probably explains why the group was so short-lived. For example, Hélion did not consider Daura an abstract painter, and thought that he should not be a member of the group. For his part, a few weeks before the exhibition opened, Daura wrote to Seuphor saying that he would not show with the group, because his work was not ready. Seuphor remedied this crisis by telling Daura that he should present something, even if it were not a new work, and that he could not pull out at this point because his name was already in the catalogue.[54]

Michel Seuphor was responsible for publication of the review *Cercle et Carré*. The first issue, which came out on March 15, 1930, contained a short paragraph by each of the group members summarizing his philosophy. Daura wrote: "Obviously, it is not the 'little errors' that distance us from 'Truth'. In any event, neither do they bring us any nearer to it. That is why I prefer the 'little truths' which are fundamental in principle. I do not believe that their elementary nature makes them childish."[55] The search for truth through art was a constant in Daura's work.

Seuphor managed to publish three issues of the review, but the group had dissolved by the end of 1930. Years later, Torres-García, by then in Montevideo where he had settled in 1934, published three issues of a review called *Círculo y Cuadrado*, for which he used the emblem designed by Daura.[56]

Ten works by Daura, all entitled *Composition*, and all probably close to abstract, were included in the first exhibition of the Surindépendants, in Paris, October 26 to November 25, 1929. Torres-García and van Doesburg used the

**Bookcover.** 1929.
Mixed media on paper, 47.9 x 31.5 cm.
MNAC, Barcelona. Photograph: Calveras, Mérida, Sagristà.

**Some members of the group Cercle et Carré, and friends.**
Left to right: Francisca Clausen, Florence Henry, Mme Torres-García, Joaquín Torres-García, Piet Mondrian, Jean Arp, Pierre Daura, Marcelle Cahn, Sophie Taeuber-Arp, Michel Seuphor, Vordemberge-Gildewart, Vera Idelson, Luigi Russolo, Mme N. Kandinsky, G. Vandongerloo, W. Kandinsky , J. Gorin.

same title for some of their works in the same exhibition. In 1930, Daura took part in the Expositions Sélectes d'Art Contemporain, organized by van Doesburg, in Holland. On this occasion, his work was shown alongside that of Torres-García, Arp, Miró, Picasso, Mondrian, Luis Fernández, and others.

It often took Daura days to compose — or rather, to construct — a work. His diary is full of mathematical formulas which he used to achieve an artistic visual balance of forms and colors on a canvas. This was an exercise of forced concentration for an artist like Daura, who so admired nature that he could paint it instinctively, structuring landscapes effortlessly in his mind. His commitment to abstraction did not last very long, although his experiments with it continued all his life. He felt more comfortable with, and enjoyed doing, figurative art.

The Dauras had decided to leave Paris, to get away from the constant social whirl, from exhibition openings, and from the continual interruptions of their artist neighbors. They wanted a house in the country, where it was quiet, where living was cheaper and where it was healthier for children, for they planned on a family. During their trip to Tarragona, the Dauras had found a plot of land near Alta-fulla with a house, an olive oil mill, a pond and a garden. They could buy the property with the money that Louise's family had sent them as a wedding present, but when they went to sign the contract, the owner, who had learned that Louise was American, demanded three times the previously agreed price.[57] They were crushed, but Daura remembered St. Cirq Lapopie, the medieval village in the Lot valley, near Cahors, which he had visited by chance in 1914. The village, with its impressive fortified church, seemed to be suspended on a cliff towering over the Lot river. It had been a prosperous town in the fourteenth and fifteenth centuries, with a population of over 6,000 inhabitants, mainly silver and goldsmiths. When the Dauras moved there, the village had just 300 inhabitants. The majority of the houses, with their red tiled roofs and Gothic windows, were still standing, but precariously. One of the oldest houses in the village was for sale, and it just happened to be the one the Dauras liked best. This time the owner did not let them down — quite the contrary; he let them stay in another house of his while they repaired their newly purchased house to make it livable. In the summer of 1930 Daura and Louise moved to St. Cirq. A new phase in Daura's life was about to begin.

19. Joaquín Torres-García: *Historia de mi vida,* op. cit. pp. 184-198. Enric Jardí: *Torres-García*, Polígrafa, Barcelona, 1973, p. 106.

20. Letter from Daura to Torres-García, March 3, 1926, Fundación Torres-García, Montevideo. Copy of the correspondence provided by Pilar García-Sedas.

21. Letter from Daura to Torres-García, January 30, 1926, Daura Archives; and Enric Jardí: *Torres-García*, op. cit.

22. Torres-García exhibited at the Galeries Dalmau in June 1926. See Jaume Vidal i Oliveras: *Josep Dalmau. L'aventura per l'art modern*. Angle and Fundació Caixa de Manresa, Manresa, 1993.

23. Letter from Torres-García to Daura, March 7, 1926, Daura Archives.

24. Enric Jardí: *Torres-García*, op. cit., p. 106.

25. Letters from Daura to Torres-García, March 3, 1925, April 27, 1926, and May 17, 1926, Fundación Torres-García, Montevideo. Copy of the correspondence provided by Pilar García-Sedas.

26. Joaquín Torres-García: *Historia de mi vida*, op. cit. p. 192. Jean Bichier subsequently changed his name to Jean Hélion.

27. Letter from Torres-García to Daura, June 27, 1927, Daura Archives.

28. Letter from Torres-García to Daura, June 30, 1927, Daura Archives.

29. Letter from Torres-García to Daura, June 20, 1928, Daura Archives.

30. Francesc Miralles: *"Un nómada catalán", La Vanguardia*, Barcelona, March 26, 1999.

31. *5 Peintres Refusés par le Jury du Salon d'Automne*, Galerie Marck, Paris, November 3-15, 1928; *Le Monde*, Paris, November 3, 1928; *Volonté*, Paris, November 3, 1928; *Blanco y Negro*, Madrid, December 9, 1928; *Paris Midi*, Paris, November 7, 1928; *Daily Mail,* November 8, 1928; *L'Intransigeant*, Paris, November 12, 1928; *Le Cri du Jour*, Paris, November 22, 1928; *Chicago Tribune*, Paris edition, November 25, 1928; *La Nau*, Barcelona, January 26, 1929.

32. *"Ai travaillé toute la journée jusqu'à 6 hs. Mal. Pire. Je n'arriverais donc pas à réaliser ce qui est au fond de mon subconscient? Architecturer un tableau. Fuir le naturel. Clairement avoir avant tout quelque chose à dire. Je crois que les plus forts obstacles pour parvenir moi à mettre d'accord directe et exacte ma conception et la réalisation sont la technique, aprise d'abord. Ensuite d'avoir trop contemplé la nature, y avoir trop recrée mes regards en peintre justement, plutôt qu'en esthéticien… Trop en ouvrier peintre! Quant un objet quelconque était l'objet de mes observations je ne songeais point au tableau ni à sa plastique. Point non plus à un ensemble pictural. La misère m'empêchant de peintre je peignais mentalement. Touche sur touche. Voilà mon erreur tragique."* Daura diary, August 16, 1928, Daura Archives.

33. Letters from Louise to her family, November 23 and 25, 1929, Daura Archives.

34. Donald Karshan: *Csaky*, Deport 15, Paris, 1973.

35. Daura produced some extremely interesting engravings of the children of Torres-García and Manolita Piña, some of which are in the Museu Nacional d'Art de Catalunya, Barcelona.

36. *"Torres-García has become even more abstract, and has influenced a large number of his satellites."* Letter from Louise to her family, July 11, 1929, Daura Archives.

37. *Togores. Classicisme i renovació (obra de 1914 a 1931),* Museo Reina Sofia - Museu d'Art Modern de MNAC, Madrid-Barcelona, November 1997-April 1998; *Un altre aspecte de Josep de Togores. Pintures de l'època de Paris 1928 -1930*, Ianua, Barcelona, 1975.

38. The sketches for the Altafulla fresco, which was never done, are at the Museu Nacional d'Art de Catalunya. It is not known if the second fresco was made. On the death of Carles Albesa, an obituary was published praising Albesa's designs, which in fact were Daura's. See Àngel Fernández: *Mirador*, Barcelona, July 30, 1931, p. 7. In a letter to her family, Louise also commented on this false attribution; July 6, 1931, Daura Archives.

39. J.Torres-García: "Pere Daura", *La Veu de Catalunya*, Barcelona, June 22, 1929.

40. The article was about the Architecture Exhibition which had been held at the Galeries Dalmau, in April 1929.

41. An engraving of Albert Junyent, done by Daura in Paris in 1930, is in the Museu Nacional d'Art de Catalunya, Barcelona.

42. Letters from Louise to her family, February 14 and May 26, 1930, Daura Archives.

43. *Exposición de arte moderno nacional y extranjero*, Catalogue, Galeries Dalmau, Barcelona, 1929.

44. Letter from Louise to her family, September 17, 1929, Daura Archives.

45. Eliseu Trenc: "Cercle et Carré", *Avui*, Barcelona, November 14, 1996.

46. Letter from Louise to her mother, December 29, 1929, Daura Archives.

47. *"4 h. avec les T. G., partis chez Seuphor. Reçus très cordialement. Avons essayé de définir la possible création d'un groupe tous ceux qui travaillent dans le constructivisme. Mondrian en tête...."* Daura diary, November 24, 1929, Daura Archives.

48. Daura diary, December 13, 1929, Daura Archives.

49. *"A fin d'éviter de rapports désagréables on a cru necessaire ce groupe fut divisé en deux sections A et B. L'antipatie de Torres pour Engel, Hélion et Wants l'ayant exigé."* Daura diary, November 24, 1929, Daura Archives.

50. Letter from Louise to her family, December 7, 1929, Daura Archives.

51. Michel Seuphor: *Le Style et le Cri*, Editions du Seuil, Paris, 1965.

52. *"Voulez-vous demander à Daura qu'il desinne notre enseigne (le nom de la revue) sur un papier grand comme celui-ci. Il a l'habitude de ces choses me semble-t-il. Ça devrer être fait au plus vite…. J'aimerais cependant en toute chose demander votre avis ainsi que celui de Daura. A 3 on est plus intelligent que seul…. Je passe chez vous et (ou) chez Daura mercredi 25 à 3 h. pour prendre le dessin de Daura…."* Letter from Seuphor to Torres-García, December 21, 1929, Archives of American Art, Washington D. C.

53. On November 30, 1929, Daura was commissioned to design the cover of the Italian edition, on which he worked December 2, 3 and 4, 1929. Daura diary, Daura Archives.

54. Letter from Seuphor to Daura, April 14, 1930, Daura Archives.

55. *"Ce ne sont pas les 'petites erreurs' qui nous éloignent de la 'Vérité', évidemment. En tout cas, elles ne nous en rapprochent point non plus. C'est pourquoi je leur préfère les 'petites vérités', qui, elles, sont fondamentales en principe. Je ne crois pas que leur valeur élémentaire les rende pour cela enfantines."* Cercle et Carré, Paris, No. 1, March 15, 1930.

56. *Cercle et Carré. Revista de la Asociación de Arte Constructivo*, Montevideo, Uruguay, Second period, No. 1, May 1936, No. 2, February 1937 and No. 3, September 1937.

57. Letter from Louise to her sister, Lelia Northrop, May 5, 1929, Daura Archives.

**L'Eglise à Collioure.** ca. 1925.
Oil on canvas, 54 x 63 cm.
Musée Hyacinthe Rigaud, Perpignan. Photograph: Michel Jauze.

**Collioure.** ca. 1927.
Oil on canvas, 54 x 65 cm.
Private collection. Photograph: Martí Gasull.

**Port of Cassis.** 1927.
Oil on canvas, 46 x 55 cm.
Private collection. Photograph: Martí Gasull.

**Still life.** 1925.
Oil on canvas, 60 x 38 cm.
MNAC, Barcelona. Photograph: Calveras, Mérida, Sagristà.

**Still life.** ca. 1925.
Oil on canvas, 23 x 43 cm.
Martha Daura collection, 2170. Photograph: Paige Critcher.

**Still life.** 1924.
Gouache on paper, 22 x 30 cm.
MNAC, Barcelona. Photograph: Calveras, Mérida, Sagristà.

**Still life.** 1924-30.
Oil on canvas, 38 x 55 cm.
Museu Diocesà de Menorca, Ciutadella. Photograph: Cisco Moll.

**Still life.** 1929.
Oil on canvas, 42 x 49 cm.
Sala d'Art Artur Ramon, Barcelona. Photograph: Martí Gasull.

**Tea Service.** ca. 1928.
Gouache on paper, 44 x 66 cm.
Musée des Augustins, Toulouse.

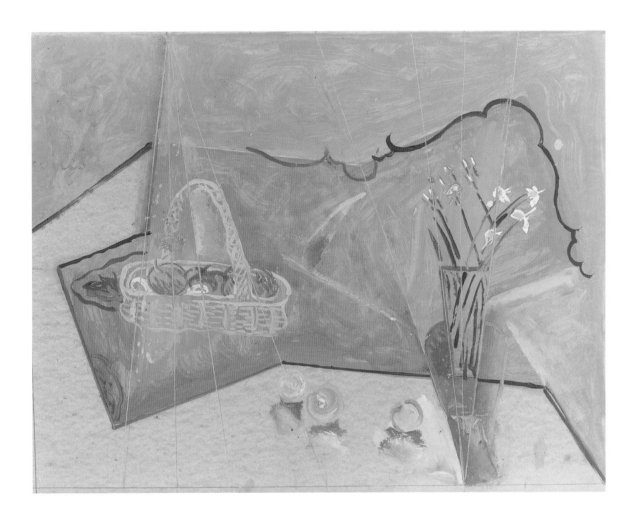

**Still life**. 1927-29.
Gouache on paper, 26 x 35 cm.
Private collection. Photograph: Martí Gasull.

**Still life.** 1927-29.
Mixed media on paper, 54.5 x 74.5 cm.
MNAC, Barcelona. Photograph: Calveras, Mérida, Sagristà.

**Portrait.** 1925-30.
Oil on canvas, 54 x 45.5 cm.
Private collection. Photograph: Marti Gasull.

**Self-portrait.** ca. 1925.
Pencil and ink on paper, 28.1 x 21.6 cm.
MNAC, Barcelona. Photograph: Calveras, Mérida, Sagristà.

**Pour être elegant.** ca. 1924.
Mixed media on paper, 10 x 33 cm.
MNAC, Barcelona. Photograph: Calveras, Mérida, Sagristà.

**Floral Motif.** ca. 1925.
Mixed media on cardboard, 21.4 x 28.3 cm.
MNAC, Barcelona. Photograph: Calveras, Mérida, Sagristà.

**Self-portrait.** ca. 1932.
Etching,15.8 x 12 cm.
MNAC, Barcelona. Photograph: Calveras, Mérida, Sagristà.

**Self-portrait.** ca. 1932.
Etching, 13.4 x 11 cm.
MNAC, Barcelona. Photograph: Calveras, Mérida, Sagristà.

**Mythological Scene.** 1920-30.
Etching, 13 x 18 cm.
MNAC, Barcelona. Photograph: Calveras, Mérida, Sagristà.

**Caravan.** 1920-30.
Linoleum, 12 x 24.5 cm.
MNAC, Barcelona. Photograph: Calveras, Mérida, Sagristà.

**King of Hearts.** 1920-26.
Mixed media on paper, 20.5 x 13.2 cm.
MNAC, Barcelona.
Photograph: Calveras, Mérida, Sagristà.

**Three of Hearts.** 1920-26.
Mixed media on paper, 18.5 x 11.7 cm.
MNAC, Barcelona.
Photograph: Calveras, Mérida, Sagristà.

**Xavier Benguerel.** 1930.
Etching, 13 x 18 cm.
MNAC, Barcelona. Photograph: Calveras, Mérida, Sagristà.

**Child in Sailor Collar.** ca. 1930.
Etching, 9 x 6.6 cm.
MNAC, Barcelona. Photograph: Calveras, Mérida, Sagristà.

**Portrait.** 1925-30.
Oil on paper, 64 x 49 cm.
Musée de Figeac. Photograph: Nelly Blaya.

**Portrait.** 1926.
Oil on paper, 51 x 66 cm.
Musée de Figeac. Photograph: Nelly Blaya.

**Portrait.** 1925.
Oil on canvas, 81 x 65 cm.
Museu Diocesà de Menorca, Ciutadella. Photograph: Cisco Moll.

**Portrait**. ca. 1925.
Oil on canvas, 81 x 60 cm.
Museu Diocesà de Menorca, Ciutadella. Photograph: Cisco Moll.

**Louise in Red Beret.** ca. 1928.
Oil on canvas, 65 x 50 cm.
Musée Hyacinthe Rigaud, Perpignan. Photograph: Michel Jauze.

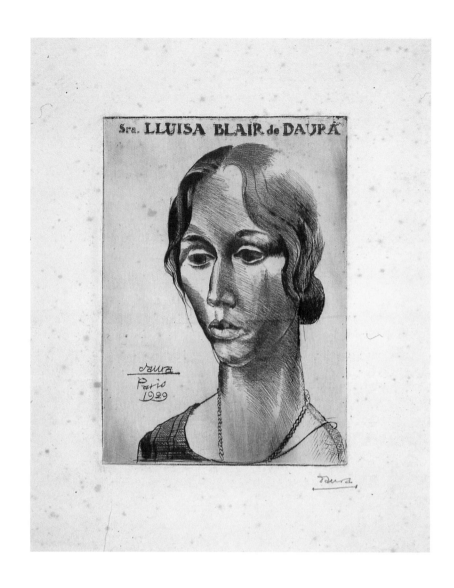

**Sra. Lluisa Blair de Daura.** 1929.
Etching, 18 x 13 cm.
MNAC, Barcelona. Photograph: Calveras, Mérida, Sagristà.

**Nudes.** 1930-35.
Oil on cardboard, 24 x 50 cm. Musée Hyacinthe Rigaud, Perpignan. Photograph: Michel Jauze.

**Louise Heron Blair.** 1928.
Charcoal and pencil on paper, 18 x 13 cm. MNAC, Barcelona. Photograph: Calveras, Mérida, Sagristà.

**Nude**. ca. 1930.
Mixed media on paper, 32 x 25.5 cm.
MNAC, Barcelona. Photograph: Calveras, Mérida, Sagristà.

**Two Children.** 1925-28.
Mixed media on paper, 35 x 42.8 cm.
MNAC, Barcelona. Photograph: Calveras, Mérida, Sagristà.

**Bay of Cargese.** Corsica. 1928.
Oil on canvas, 81 x 99 cm.
Abadia de Montserrat, Museu de Montserrat, 201.358. Photograph: Lluís Casals.

**Piana Golfe.** Corsica. 1928.
Oil on canvas, 65 x 50 cm.
Musée Hyacinthe Rigaud, Perpignan. Photograph: Michel Jauze.

**Maison du Troubadour Maestrale.** Corsica. 1928.
Oil on canvas, 68 x 81 cm.
MNAC, Barcelona. Photograph: Calveras, Mérida, Sagristà.

**Maison Spinoza a Porto.** Corsica. 1928.
Oil on canvas, 59 x 71.5 cm.
Private collection. Photograph: Martí Gasull.

**Farmyard at Cargese.** Corsica. 1928.
Gouache on paper, 40 x 52 cm.
Martha Daura collection, 2058. Photograph: Paige Critcher.

**Ajaccio**. Corsica. 1928.
Gouache on paper, 65 x 50 cm.
Musée Paul Dupuy, Toulouse.

**Fountain at Cargese.** Corsica. 1928.
Oil on paper, 71 x 51 cm.
Martha Daura collection, 2059. Photograph: Paige Critcher.

**Bay.** Corsica. 1928.
Gouache on paper, 50 x 65 cm.
Martha Daura collection, 2018. Photograph: Paige Critcher.

**Room at Cargese.** Corsica. 1928.
Gouache on paper, 59 x 45 cm.
Musée Hyacinthe Rigaud, Perpignan. Photograph: Michel Jauze.

**August Torres.** 1929.
Etching, 18 x 13 cm.
MNAC, Barcelona. Photograph: Calveras, Mérida, Sagristà.

**Altafulla**. 1929.
Oil on canvas, 60 x 73 cm.
Abadia de Montserrat, Museu de Montserrat, 201.355. Photograph: Lluís Casals.

**Untitled.** 1929.
Oil on paper, 38.2 x 46.2 cm.
MACBA, Barcelona. Photograph: Rocco Ricci.

BETWEEN REPRESENTATION AND ABSTRACTION

**Still life.** 1931-39.
Oil on wood, 41 x 55 cm.
Museu Diocesà de Menorca, Ciutadella. Photograph: Cisco Moll.

**Still life.** 1924 -30.
Gouache and oil on paper, 49 x 64 cm.
MNAC, Barcelona. Photograph: Calveras, Mérida, Sagristà.

**Still life.** 1930.
Oil on canvas, 23 x 28 cm.
MNAC, Barcelona. Photograph: Calveras, Mérida, Sagristà.

**Still life.** ca. 1928.
Oil on paper, 50 x 65 cm.
MNAC, Barcelona. Photograph: Calveras, Mérida, Sagristà.

**Female Torso.** 1930.
Oil on canvas, 46 x 38 cm.
Centre Georges Pompidou, Paris. Photograph: Adam Rzepka.

**Still life.** ca. 1929.
Oil on paper, 46 x 55 cm.
Centre Georges Pompidou, Paris. Photograph: Adam Rzepka.

**Nature Morte.** ca. 1929.
Oil on canvas, 38 x 46 cm.
MNAC, Barcelona. Photograph: Calveras, Mérida, Sagristà.

**Female Head.** 1929.
Oil on canvas, 46.3 x 38.1 cm.
MACBA, Barcelona. Photograph: Rocco Ricci.

**Still life.** 1929.
Oil on canvas, 38.2 x 46 cm.
MACBA, Barcelona. Photograph: Rocco Ricci.

**Still life.** 1929.
Oil on paper, 38.3 x 46.4 cm.
MACBA, Barcelona. Photograph: Rocco Ricci.

**Still life.** ca. 1929.
Oil on canvas, 22 x 27 cm.
Martha Daura collection, 2231. Photograph: Paige Critcher.

**Untitled.** ca. 1929.
Oil on canvas, 24 x 33 cm.
Centre Georges Pompidou, Paris. Photograph: Adam Rzepka.

**Self-portrait in Mauve**.1930-35.
Oil on canvas, 42 x 34 cm.
Abadia de Montserrat, Museu de Montserrat, 201.358. Photograph: Manuel Pérez.

**Lot River in Autumn.** St. Cirq Lapopie. 1930-36.
Oil on canvas, 54 x 65 cm.
MNAC, Barcelona. Photograph: Calveras, Mérida, Sagristà.

**Up to the Church.** St. Cirq Lapopie. 1930.
Etching, 52 x 37 cm.
Musée Paul Dupuy. Toulouse.

**Church. St. Cirq Lapopie.** 1938.
Oil on canvas, 82.5 x 65.8 cm.
Museu Diocesà de Menorca. Ciutadella. Photograph: Cisco Moll.

**Louise Holding Martha.** ca. 1933.
Ink on paper, 36.3 x 25.2 cm.
MNAC, Barcelona. Photograph: Calveras, Mérida, Sagristà.

the colors of autumn, fascinated Daura, and for a while the Appalachian Mountains became the principal subject of his work.

During his trip to the U.S., Daura visited New York twice, in August 1934 and in May 1935. He went to exhibitions of the works of his friends Charles Logasa, Torres-García and Jean Hélion, and saw again John Xceron and Francesc Duran i Reynals. He had thought of renting a studio, but changed his mind on seeing how badly artists were paid and how poor the market was. In Tarrytown, New York, he took part in a group show with one of his landscapes.[77]

In September 1935, Daura returned to St. Cirq, a month before Martha and Louise, in order to prepare the exhibition of his Virginia landscapes which Modest Sabaté was organizing for him at Barcelona's Sala Barcino.[78] The critics continued to be favorable: "His success with a vivacious and passionate style is total. As a result, Pere Daura's paintings, magnificent expressions of color, are of insuperable merit."[79]

58. Elizabeth Hollister Frost: *The Wedding Ring*, Coward McCann, Inc., New York, 1939. Daura illustrated two more of the author's works: *This Side of Land*, Coward McCann, Inc., New York, 1942, and "The Painter of La Popie", *Tomorrow*, New York, September, 1944.

59. Letter from Louise to her family, November 1, 1931, Daura Archives. "Montserrat vist pels artistes", *La Veu de Catalunya*, Barcelona, October 24, 1931.

60. *1ère Exposition de Peinture et Sculpture Organisée par la Casa de Catalunya (Foyer Catalan de Paris)*, Pierre Vorms editeur, Galerie Billiet, Paris, June 26 to July 9, 1931. A. Lesbats: *Le Populaire,* Paris, July 1, 1931.

61. *Exposició col·lectiva de Pintura i Escultura*, Sala Badrinas, Barcelona, Christmas-Epiphany 1931-1932.

62. *Exposició de Primavera, Saló de Montjuïc*, Palau Nacional, Barcelona, May 22 to July 3, 1932.

63. One of these drawings by Daura was purchased by the Committee of the Museums Board; letter from Montserrat Isern of the Committee to Daura, July 29, 1933, Daura Archives. The drawing is at the Museu Nacional d'Art de Catalunya in Barcelona, museum number 26.953.

64. Jean Gayrac: "Exposition Pierre Daura au Musée de Cahors", *Journal du Lot*, Cahors, November 4, 1932.

65. *Pere Daura*, Signo Club, Rosario, September 1932.

66. Carles Capdevila: "El Pintor Pere Daura", *La Publicitat*, Barcelona, December 4, 1932. Ràfols: "Pere Daura", *El Matí*, Barcelona, December 8, 1932.

67. J. C. i V.: "Pere Daura", *L'Opinió*, Barcelona, December 3, 1932.

68. *Exposition d'Art Moderne Catalan*, Amsterdam, 1933.

69. A landscape of St. Cirq was purchased by the Figeac Town Council; letter from Louise to her family, November 19, 1933, Daura Archives. It still hangs in one of the rooms of the Town Hall of Figeac.

70. Enric F. Gual: "Saló de Montjuïc", *Mirador*, Barcelona, June 8, 1933, p. 7.

71. For reasons of which I am unaware, this work does not appear in the catalogue of acquisitions of the Museums Board, or of the Museu d'Art Modern in Barcelona.

72. Modest Sabaté: "L'exposició Pere Daura a les Galeries Syra", *La Veu de Catalunya*, Barcelona, December 13, 1933.

73. Letter from Louise to her family, December 18, 1933, Daura Archives.

74. Letter from Daura to Louise, October 27, 1933, Daura Archives.

75. I have not been able to confirm whether this exhibition was actually held.

76. Letter from Daura to Mr. Rachou, August 11, 1933, Daura Archives.

77. "Local Artist Will Exhibit at Institute", *Daily News*, Tarrytown, April 26, 1935.

78. *Pere Daura. Exposició*, Sala Barcino, Barcelona, December 14-27, 1935. Andrenius [Modest Sabaté]: "Una conversa amb el pintor Pere Daura", *La Veu de Catalunya,* Barcelona, December 1, 1932. E. Clivillés: "Pere Daura", *Esplai,* Barcelona, December 22, 1935.

79. E. Clivillés: "La pintura de Pere Daura", *El Matí*, Barcelona, December 18, 1935.

**Little Martha Sleeping.** 1937.
Pencil on paper, 24.7 x 17 cm.
MNAC, Barcelona. Photograph: Calveras, Mérida, Sagristà.

vera, at the Saló de Montjuïc, with a still life, a landscape of St. Cirq and a portrait of a Majorcan woman.[62] He entered some drawings in the Drawing Fair at the Galeria Syra in Barcelona.[63] There were also one-man shows in 1932, as follows: Musée de Cahors, France, landscapes of St. Cirq and Corsica, portraits and abstracts;[64] Signo Club, Rosario, Argentina, landscapes of Tarragona, Majorca and Paris;[65] Galeria Syra, Barcelona, works after 1915, street scenes of Paris, landscapes of Montserrat, Majorca, St. Cirq and Altafulla, still lifes and portraits.[66]

Most of the works Daura exhibited in 1932 emphasized structure and color. Some critics praised his use of color and called him a "fauvist"; another suggested a "regression" in his work due to his flirtation with "non-representative abstraction, so far from what his strong temperament, his painter's sensitivity to the deep sensuality of matter and to the reality of the visible world, called for".[67]

At an exhibition of Catalan painters and sculptors in Amsterdam, in 1933, which included P. Créixams, Domènec Carles, Salvador Dalí, Joaquim Mir, Gargallo, Manolo and Josep Llorens Artigas, Daura showed a landscape of St. Cirq

and a still life.[68] He entered a landscape in an exhibition of modern Spanish art at the Lyon Fair, and he had five works (oils and engravings) in a Fine Arts Exhibition organized by the Town Council of Figeac, France.[69]

Daura's works shown in Barcelona at the 1933 Saló de Montjuïc, in the Exposició de Primavera, were well received: "Daura's canvases are an excellent expression of this painter's vision. Daura has superb judgment of color; rich touches sensitively focused permit us to enjoy works that are true fine art. Daura's work is another center of attraction in this spring salon."[70] One of Daura's works in the Exposició de Primavera was purchased by the Acquisitions Board of the Saló de Montjuïc.[71]

Daura entered two works in the Exposició del Nu (Exhibition of Nudes), December 1933 in Barcelona, organized by the Cercle Artístic. At the same time he had a solo show of twenty-four paintings at the Galeries d'Art Syra in Barcelona, among which were the outstanding landscapes of Majorca and St. Cirq: "landscapes which, because of the excellence of his palette, their balanced structure, their harmonious tones, match the finest art of our country's best painters."[72] The painting reproduced on the cover of the catalogue of the Syra exhibition, a view of St. Cirq in the snow, was purchased by the collector Lluís Plandiura.[73]

Yet, despite his success, Daura was not satisfied with his work. He thought that his dissatisfaction stemmed from "the difference between my intellect — consciousness or intelligence — and my subconscious and temperament. My intellect acts in the name of order, of harmony, of peace and serenity, all that is characteristic of lasting, static things. Yet my temperament reacts according to the impulse of the moment, to things that move and change. This dynamic is what gives my paintings their tragic aspect."[74] Perhaps the dynamic that Daura refers to explains why he alternately produced works emphasizing forceful structural forms and color contrasts, and other more lyrical ones with muted colors and forms.

In 1933, the Barcelona City Council and the Regional Government of Catalonia commissioned Daura to organize an Exhibition of Occitan Art in Barcelona, which was to balance a corresponding exhibition of Catalan art in Toulouse. The purpose of the exhibition[75] was to "bring together the two 'Catalonias', two cultures politically separated, but very similar in origin".[76]

In May 1934, the Dauras went to Virginia so that Pierre and Martha could meet the American side of the family. The mountains and valleys of Western Virginia, particularly with

# RETURN TO REPRESENTATION: ST. CIRQ LAPOPIE

When Daura changed his home from Paris to St. Cirq, his art (which emerged strengthened from its period of abstraction) also underwent a change. Its structure became more forceful, and its color freer. The houses, streets, cliffs and inhabitants of the medieval village became one of the main themes of both his paintings and engravings. The village was the setting for a series of short stories written by his sister-in-law, Elizabeth Hollister Frost, which Daura illustrated with engravings.[58] Engraving is a medium which Daura used extensively during the twenties and thirties. He had a firm, clear line that allowed him to do portraits and landscapes on copper plate with outstanding results. He executed the entire process, engraving and printing, in his own studio in his home.

A monumental change in the lives of Pierre and Louise came with the birth of their only child, Martha, in September 1930. The little girl became an adored model for both parents.

The art of Louise Blair should be the subject of another book, but one specific example of her work must be mentioned: a self-portrait with Spanish mantilla, at the Musée Hyacinthe Rigaud in Perpignan. It is interesting to compare this work, probably painted in 1930, to a similar portrait of Louise, in the same mantilla, painted by Daura at about the same time.

In the spring of 1931, Daura spent a few weeks painting at the Monastery of Montserrat, for the competition "Montserrat as seen by artists". Daura was awarded the St. Cecilia prize, but the competition had led to a conflict between painters who had remained in Catalonia and those who had moved elsewhere, and this affected the voting. Rafael Benet explained to Daura that in the first ballot, he had been the clear winner, but that another vote was taken to satisfy protests raised against the "traitors" who had settled outside Catalonia.[59] Daura lost the first prize, and its ten thousand pesetas which would have allowed the Dauras to travel to the U.S. to meet Louise's family. The four thousand pesetas of

**Daura in the kitchen of his medieval house at St. Cirq.** 1950s.
Photograph: Mopy-Maurice Charbonnières. Daura Archives.

the St. Cecilia prize only enabled them to spend the winter on Majorca, painting.

From June to July 1931, Daura participated in an exhibition organized by the Casa de Catalunya at the Galerie Billiet, in Paris.[60] Two landscapes by Daura were shown beside the work of Pere Créixams, Durancamps, Fenosa, Pau Gargallo, Juli González, Salvadó, Senabre, Joan Junyer, Manolo, Joan Miró, Picasso, Torres-García, and others. At the end of the year, he entered two landscapes of St. Cirq in a group painting and sculpture exhibition at the Sala Badrinas, in Barcelona.[61]

In 1932, he took part in Barcelona's Exposició de Prima-

**Self-portrait in Mauve**.1930-35.
Oil on canvas, 42 x 34 cm.
Abadia de Montserrat, Museu de Montserrat, 201.358. Photograph: Manuel Pérez.

**Untitled.** ca. 1929.
Oil on canvas, 24 x 33 cm.
Centre Georges Pompidou, Paris. Photograph: Adam Rzepka.

**St. Cirq Lapopie in Winter.** 1930-33.
Oil on canvas, 60 x 73 cm.
Martha Daura collection, 2288. Photograph: Benoit Petit.

**St. Cirq Lapopie.** 1930-34.
Oil on canvas, 65 x 81 cm.
Private collection. Photograph: Martí Gasull.

**Lot Valley.** ca. 1935.
Oil on canvas, 65 x 54 cm.
Private collection. Photograph: Martí Gasull.

**Martha at Table.** 1933.
Oil on canvas, 51 x 61 cm.
Martha Daura collection, 1132. Photograph: Paige Critcher.

**Martha.** 1939.
Oil on wood, 55 x 46 cm.
Museu Diocesà de Menorca, Ciutadella. Photograph: Cisco Moll.

**Louise and Martha.** ca. 1933.
Oil on canvas, 65 x 54 cm.
Museu Diocesà de Menorca, Ciutadella. Photograph: Cisco Moll.

**Louise as Mallorcan Woman.** 1932.
Oil on canvas, 99 x 81 cm.
Martha Daura collection, 1123. Photograph: Paige Critcher.

**Louise with Mantilla.** ca. 1930.
Oil on canvas, 81 x 54 cm.
Abadia de Montserrat, Museu de Montserrat, 201.359.
Photograph: Lluís Casals.

Louise Heron Blair.
**Self-portrait with Mantilla.** ca. 1930.
Oil on canvas, 60 x 38 cm.
Musée Hyacinthe Rigaud, Perpignan. Photograph: Michel Jauze.

**Path to St. Michael's.** Montserrat. 1931.
Oil on canvas, 82 x 73 cm.
Abadia de Montserrat, Museu de Montserrat, 200.259. Photograph: Manuel Pérez.

**Path to the Cave.** Montserrat. 1931.
Oil on canvas, 73 x 92 cm.
Private collection. Photograph: Jordi Nieva.

**Return to the Village.** Rockbridge Baths. ca. 1935.
Oil on canvas, 50 x 61 cm.
Abadia de Montserrat, Museu de Montserrat, 200.590. Photograph: Manuel Pérez.

**Rockbridge Baths**, ca. 1935.
Oil on canvas, 46 x 55 cm.
Museu Diocesà de Menorca, Ciutadella. Photograph: Cisco Moll.

**Milking.** Rockbridge Baths. ca. 1935.
Oil on canvas, 61 x 51 cm.
Martha Daura collection, 1002.  Photograph: Paige Critcher.

**Self-portrait.** ca. 1936.
Oil on canvas, 42 x 34 cm.
MNAC, Barcelona. Photograph: Calveras, Mérida, Sagristà.

# THE SPANISH CIVIL WAR

## ( 1936 - 1939 )

Although he lived in France, Daura never lost touch with Catalonia, and he closely followed the new direction of Spanish politics after the creation of the Republic. When the Spanish Civil War broke out in 1936, he waited anxiously, hoping for news announcing the victory of the Republic. In February 1937, now somewhat discouraged, he went to Barcelona. While he was talking to friends in the city and trying to decide how he could help the Republican cause, he learned that a forward artillery observer was needed. He enlisted.

In his forty-first year, and unable to open his left hand because of a permanent injury, he left for the front. His fellow militiamen, who were much younger, called him "grandpa". Artist friends who also joined to defend the Republic included Gustavo Cochet, Albert Junyent and Joan Junyer.

Daura was sent to the Teruel front as an artillery observer. In the letters he wrote to Louise, he described the harshness of life at the front, the cold, the hunger and the nearness of the enemy. The letters often included drawings: the tent where he slept, the lamb that became the unit mascot and which the men christened "Mosquita", his comrades, etc. He explained to Louise how he would often read from Margaret Mitchell's novel, *Gone with the Wind*, to his fellow soldiers, and how he found that the military situation of the soldiers of the Southern Army so resembled that of his Loyalist militia.[80] Daura wrote to Margaret Mitchell, explaining the situation in which he and his comrades found themselves, and she responded with a very encouraging letter.

Daura's moving letters describing his war experiences prompted Louise to translate whole paragraphs and copy them into the letters she sent to her family in the U.S. Interest in the Spanish Civil War led to the publication of some of these accounts in *The Atlantic Monthly*.[81] An Eng-

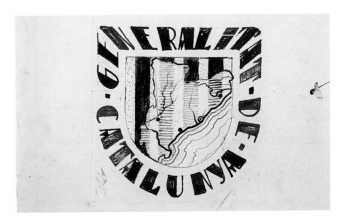

**Study for Generalitat Shield.** ca. 1933.
Mixed media on paper, 25.1 x 38.2 cm.
MNAC, Barcelona. Photograph: Calveras, Mérida, Sagristà.

lish publisher suggested that Louise write a book about the war, to be titled "Iberia Calls". On the day that Louise heard of the fall of Barcelona, she received a letter from the editors apologizing for wasting her time, and announcing that the book would not be published.

Daura remained at the front until he was wounded in the legs and the left arm. Because of the overworked hospitals and the lack of medical resources in Catalonia, he was sent back to France for further treatment and convalescence at St. Cirq. As soon as he was physically able, he began to help those who were fleeing the war. For months he took people into his home, he visited French detention camps, and he wrote letters attempting to obtain news about friends and relations. Years later, Daura was still receiving grateful letters from people he had helped to get out of the camps.[82]

His personal war experiences are poignantly illustrated in the drawings, engravings and paintings he produced from 1937 to 1939; many of these are in the Museu Nacional d'Art de Catalunya, in Barcelona. The engravings are particularly expressive, portraying his comrades and life at the front. Most of them are signed, and they often identify the

**Civil War.** 1937.
Pencil on paper, 32 x 23 cm.
MNAC, Barcelona. Photograph: Calveras, Mérida, Sagristà.

places where they were drawn — Teruel, Bronchales, Valde-cuenca, Campillo, Carbonera, etc. — and the soldiers por-trayed. They are frequently heavily worked, with dark tones which produce a dramatic effect. He also did a series of engravings called "Civilization", depicting the cruelty and absurdity of war, and the violence which affects the most innocent of all, the children.

He painted a series of self-portraits, in uniform, which vividly display both his determination to fight, and his anguish at the need. Daura is in the foreground, and in the background are scenes of the consequences of war; burning villages and deserted landscapes.

Another group of works focused on the nightmare of suf-fering he witnessed in the French detention camps. The war did not end for him when he left the front. Pain con-tinued to rack everyone who was forced into exile. These are figurative works, in which the characters seem to move in a hallucinatory atmosphere.

Daura was, above all, a romantic idealist. Time healed his physical wounds, but never those to his spirit. Like his god-father, Pablo Casals, Daura never wanted to return to Cat-alonia until a democratic political order was restored, and unfortunately, that was not until after his death.

80. Letter from Daura to Louise, March 24, 1937, Daura Archives.

81. Louise de Daura: "The Soldier Returns. Spanish Letters", *The Atlantic Monthly*, Boston, January 1938, pp. 28-34.

82. In 1941, the painter Josep Gausachs wrote to Daura from the Dominican Republic, recounting his hardships during the war and thanking Daura for vis-iting him and for lending him money, June 2, 1941, Daura Archives.

**Civil War.** Carboneras. June 1937.
Pencil on paper, 23 x 32 cm.
MNAC, Barcelona. Photograph: Calveras, Mérida, Sagristà.

**Civil War**. Teruel. March 1937.
Pencil on paper, 32 x 23 cm.
MNAC, Barcelona. Photograph: Calveras, Mérida, Sagristà.

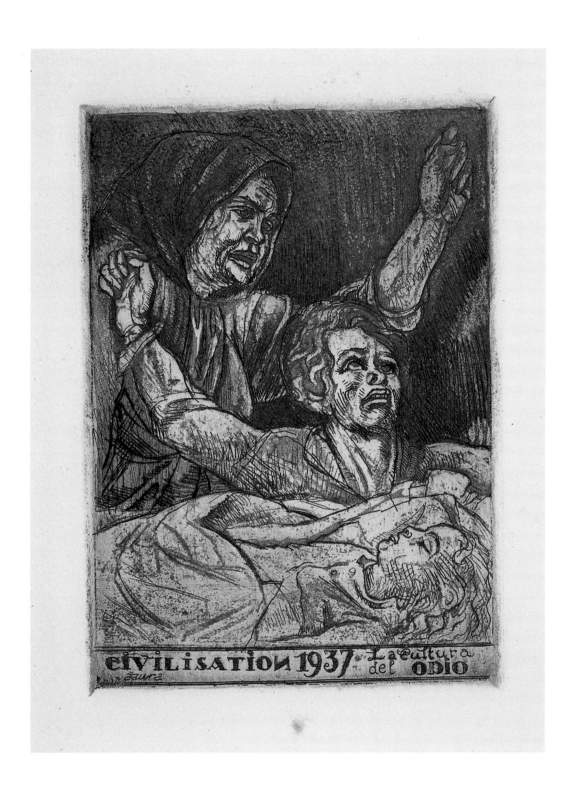

**Civil War. Civilisation, La cultura del odio.** 1937.
Etching, 25 x 18 cm.
MNAC, Barcelona. Photograph: Calveras, Mérida, Sagristà.

**Le Cauchemar**. Argelès s/Mer. 1939.
Oil on canvas, 59 x 72 cm.
MNAC, Barcelona. Photograph: Calveras, Mérida, Sagristà.

**Argelès.** 1939.
Oil on canvas, 46 x 33 cm.
Musée Hyacinthe Rigaud, Perpignan. Photograph: Michel Jauze

**Civil War.** 1938-39.
Pencil and watercolor on paper, 24 x 32 cm.
MNAC, Barcelona. Photograph: Calveras, Mérida, Sagristà.

**War.** 1939-42.
Oil on wood, 74 x 90 cm.
Martha Daura collection, 1333.  Photograph: Paige Critcher.

**Self-portrait in Militia Uniform.** ca. 1938.
Oil on canvas, 65 x 54 cm.
MNAC, Barcelona. Photograph: Calveras, Mérida, Sagristà.

**Self-portrait in Militia Uniform.** ca. 1938.
Oil on wood, 66 x 54 cm.
Museu Diocesà de Menorca, Ciutadella. Photograph: Cisco Moll.

**Self-portrait as Painter.** 1940.
Oil on wood, 61 x 46 cm.
Museu Diocesà de Menorca, Ciutadella. Photograph: Cisco Moll.

# A NEW LIFE: VIRGINIA

**Daura at the opening of his first Lynchburg exhibition,**
December 7, 1941. Photograph: Howard Hammersley. Daura Archives.

In the spring of 1939, Louise became ill. The doctors in Paris diagnosed a serious kidney problem and recommended that she go to the U.S., where there were specialists who could offer the latest treatment. Time was crucial, and on the very next day, the Dauras sailed for America on a journey which they little suspected would keep them away from Europe for many years. Happily, Louise's symptoms were not those of the serious illness she had been diagnosed as having in Paris, and she recovered quickly. However, while the Dauras were in Virginia, World War II broke out.

Daura had refused to return to Spain — with the consequence that his Spanish nationality was revoked — and the family could not return to France until the war in Europe was over. Daura and his daughter Martha became naturalized U.S. citizens in 1943.

The Dauras settled at Rockbridge Baths, Virginia, in a summer home belonging to Louise's family, on the very property where the Baths (the warm springs) are located. The rolling landscapes of Virginia, with its farms, barns, cattle and farm workers, provided a new inspiration for Daura's works. In 1940, he spent a few weeks on Nantucket, an island off the coast of Massachusetts, where he painted landscapes of the windswept island.

The work Daura produced in Virginia quickly came to public attention in a series of group exhibitions. In the autumn of 1940, he exhibited landscapes of Rockbridge Baths and St. Cirq in Richmond and Hopewell.

In his first solo show, held at the Lynchburg Art Gallery, Daura presented over one hundred works: oils, temperas and drawings; landscapes of Nantucket and Rockbridge Baths, scenes of the Spanish Civil War, self-portraits and other portraits. On the day the exhibition opened, December 7, 1941, the Japanese bombed Pearl Harbor and the U.S. entered the war. Once again, war cast its shadow over the painter's life.

In 1942, two war posters, entitled "Deliver Us from Evil", which Daura had entered in a competition, were selected by New York's Museum of Modern Art as part of a traveling exhibition. The same year, Daura was commissioned to organize an exhibition of his own work and that of his brother-in-law, the French painter Jean Hélion, who was then a German prisoner. Hélion's works were mainly abstract, while Daura's were landscapes of Nantucket and Virginia, still lifes and portraits. The exhibition catalogue emphasized the space, color and harmony of Hélion's work; it characterized Daura as an ally of nature, pointing out his studies of the same place from different angles and at different times of day.[83] From 1942 to 1945, the Dauras lived

**Daura and Louise.** Virginia. ca. 1945.
Daura Archives.

in the fifties. He sculpted in wood, stone, and occasionally metal. He even tried paper pulp.[86] Most of his sculptures have a figurative origin, although a few are abstract geometrical forms. Daura's sculptures cannot be classified as belonging to a particular movement. They include representational works, more abstract works, with concave and convex surfaces, reminiscent of cubism, and schematic works which recall primitive sculpture. Usually it was the texture and shape of the wood or stone which suggested the subject.

Another new feature of Daura's art was the introduction of religious themes, beginning with works of the Spanish Civil War. The figures are often shown in prayerful attitudes, and the artist seems to liken the death of innocents to the death of Christ on the Cross. Daura had previously done religious work for the decoration of a church (scenes from the life of Saint Francis for Tarragona), or of his house in St. Cirq (scenes from the life of Saint Martha which he painted in the stairway). A work included in Daura's solo exhibition in Lynchburg, in 1941, shows the figure of a soldier representing brute force, attacking two women and a child; there is a crucifix in the background, in an allusion to innocent death at the hands of aggression. In the late forties, Daura's themes included the Crucifixion, Pietas, the Holy Family and, above all, mother figures. Daura, who lost his mother before he was eight, felt that the figure of the mother, who gives her life to make another one possible, is the ultimate symbol of creation and existence:

*"It's always the mother and the child. Nobody has been able to explain the gift she gives. No intellectual has been able to explain: everything turns to the mother and child."*[87]

Daura had a solo show at the Lynchburg Art Center in 1953. He exhibited sculptures, drawings, watercolors and oils: portraits, landscapes from the twenties and thirties of Majorca and Tarragona, Corsica and St. Cirq, and recent works done in Virginia.[88]

During his Lynchburg period, Daura restored paintings and painted portraits on commission to supplement his income. His official job, however, was teaching studio art, and his personal undertaking was helping his students and the public to understand art in all its aspects, helping young painters realize that they are not in possession of "the truth" and that they must respect other artistic choices: *"Because we remain blind to all unknown things we must remember that our truth is only a part of the truth if truth at all."*[89] *"A large part of an education in the appreciation of the art of other people consists in breaking down the rigidity of a*

on a property called "Tuckaway", with a lovely eighteenth-century house which a friend, Colonel Tucker, had offered them when he was recalled to military service. The nearby hills and barns became frequent subjects of Daura's paintings.

The Dauras moved to an apartment in Lynchburg, Virginia, in 1945. Martha had by now reached university age, which meant extra expense for the painter. To earn more money, Daura became an art teacher. During the 1945-1946 academic year, Daura was Chairman of the Art Department of Lynchburg College. The following autumn, he joined the staff of Randolph-Macon Woman's College, also in Lynchburg, where he taught for seven years, until 1953.

Daura combined his teaching with exhibitions. In 1950, he exhibited two landscapes, one of Majorca and one of Corsica, and five sculptures in the 39th Contemporary American Exhibition of Painting and Sculpture, organized by Randolph-Macon.[84] This selection, and the works he showed the following year — two sculptures (*Crucifixion* and *Beam end*) and an abstract (*Illusion of Depth*) —[85] point to a change in the direction of Daura's work. Sculpture was the new art form Daura adopted enthusiastically

**Daura retouching sculpture of St. John the Baptist.** 1953. Daura Archives.

*man's own local cultural ideals — turning him from a sort of provincial robot into a human being.*"[90]

Educational institutions and professional groups often called on Daura to speak about art, and newspapers and magazines asked him to contribute articles. All of his writings and notes reflect a scholarly approach. The meaning of art and man's intimate relation with it, as a means of expression since the dawn of antiquity are two of the themes about which he most often wrote and spoke. Often there would be audiences with whom he could take nothing for granted, and who would question everything: "*Art is a message, an inner message no words can define, but words and forms and sounds can carry and give it to the world. Always art is a give away gesture, art is a generous impulse's product.*"[91] "*Art has been and always is the means and the purpose of the irresistible urge for self-expression, expression of those values or beliefs latent in man, which establish the link between man and the ever receding over yonder.*"[92] "*Dedica-*

*tion to art, practice of art, keeps its equal place side by side with these magical 'myths', these 'beliefs' that have been and are the living forces directing man towards his destiny.... Religion, Flag, Love, Happiness, Home.*"[93]

Daura often had to justify the usefulness of art. He championed the various artistic movements which existed side by side, and defended figurative art at a time when abstract expressionism and chromatic abstraction were sweeping all before them: "*When you paint, if you just listen to your inner self and remain true to it... there will always be in your work a pure esthetic content. This is what esthetics is: the expression, the mirror, the image, the figuration of the inner human feelings and sentiments as opposed to the idea of exclusive usefulness or pure abstract reason.... The tormented man of today in his thirst for certitude and security in art, as in other things of life may in an apparently contradictory sequence, give now his interest to a realist approach to painting, then shift immediately to any of the many esthetic ways in which artists have expressed themselves throughout the history of man.*"[94] Figurative art, he suggested, is the art form which responds to man's need for security. These words of Daura's anticipated the appearance of Pop Art as a form of realism, a style which emerged as a reaction to the subjectivity and ambiguity of abstract expressionism.

One of Daura's outstanding students at Randolph-Macon Woman's College was Queena Stovall,[95] a woman who joined his art class at the age of 62. Daura immediately realized that Queena had an instinctive personal style. She painted familiar country scenes, the farm and its chores, the animals, her family, and her neighbors, white and black. This highly imaginative woman had a fresh, distinctive, naive style. Daura advised Queena simply to paint, and not attend classes or study theory, lest it spoil what was most notable in her art, its spontaneity. Queena became famous as a folk artist.

83. Marie Pietri & Carolyn Smith: *Hélion & Daura*, Virginia Museum of Fine Arts, Richmond, May 12-30, 1942.

84. *The Thirty-ninth Annual Exhibition of Contemporary American Painting and Sculpture,* Randolph-Macon Woman's College Art Gallery, Lynchburg, May 7 to June 4, 1950.

85. *Paintings, Sculptures, Ceramics, & Prints, Art Faculty in Virginia Colleges,* Randolph-Macon Woman's College Art Gallery, Lynchburg, May 12 to June 4, 1951.

86. "Pierre Daura Finds Medium of Sculpture — It's Paper Pulp", *The News,* Lynchburg, April 19, 1959.

87. "Daura: A Life of Art", *The Roanoke Times*, Roanoke, December, 29, 1974.

88. *Pierre Daura*, Lynchburg Art Center, Lynchburg, November 1-15, 1953; "Lexington Artist to Open Show in Lynchburg Today", *The Roanoke Times*, Roanoke, November 1, 1953; and Lib Wiley: "Art Gallery Picks Pierre Daura for First One-man Exhibition", *The Advance*, Lynchburg, October 30, 1953.

89. Daura undated notes, Daura Archives.

90. Daura undated manuscript, Daura Archives.

91. Letter from Daura to Mrs. Moore about why people buy art, undated, Daura Archives.

92. Daura undated notebook, Daura Archives.

93. Excerpt from the text Daura wrote for the catalogue of the 25th Annual Civic Art Show of the Lynchburg Art Club, 1957.

94. Daura's notes for the lecture: "Art Can Always Be an Aesthetic Experience", undated, Daura Archives.

95. *Queena Stovall. Artist of the Blue Ridge Piedmont*, Lynchburg College, Lynchburg, April-September 1975.

**Laundry in Winter.** Rockbridge Baths. 1939-42.
Oil on wood, 46 x 61 cm.
Asheville Museum of Art, NC. Photograph: Paige Critcher.

**Autumn on the Maury.** Rockbridge Baths. 1939-50.
Oil on wood, 60 x 73 cm.
Martha Daura collection, 1012. Photograph: Paige Critcher

**Martha at Thirteen.** 1943-44.
Oil on canvas, 86 x 72 cm.
Martha Daura collection, 1138. Photograph: Paige Critcher.

**The Harp of the Winds.** Nantucket. 1940.
Oil on wood, 61 x 61 cm.
Martha Daura collection, 1059. Photograph: Paige Critcher.

**Windy Land.** Nantucket. 1940.
Oil on wood, 61 x 72 cm.
Martha Daura collection, 1060. Photograph: Paige Critcher.

**The Big Barn at Tuckaway.** Rockbridge County. 1942-45.
Oil on canvas, 66 x 82 cm.
Martha Daura collection, 1021.  Photograph: Paige Critcher.

**Tuckaway**. Rockbridge County. 1942-45.
Oil on cardboard, 46 x 61 cm.
Martha Daura collection, 1022.  Photograph: Paige Critcher.

**House Mountain.** Rockbridge County. 1942-45.
Oil on cardboard, 36 x 53 cm.
Martha Daura collection, 1024.  Photograph: Paige Critcher.

**Willows in the Mist**. Rockbridge County. 1942-45.
Oil on canvas, 56 x 64 cm.
Martha Daura collection, 1031.  Photograph: Paige Critcher.

**Lilacs and House Mountain.** Rockbridge County. 1942-45.
Oil on canvas, 67 x 81 cm.
St. Petersburg Museum of Fine Arts, FL.

**Autumn Trees.** Rockbridge Baths. 1945-55.
Tempera on paper, 55 x 75 cm.
Martha Daura collection, 4691. Photograph: Paige Critcher.

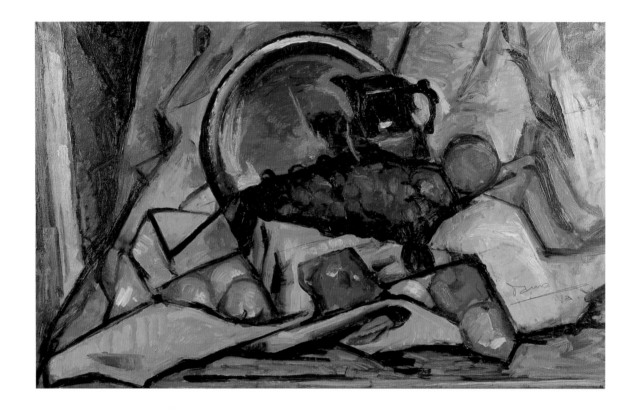

**Still life.** 1950-65.
Oil on paper, 50 x 91 cm.
Martha Daura collection, 1297. Photograph: Paige Critcher.

**Still life.** 1961-71.
Oil on canvas, 41 x 61 cm.
Martha Daura collection, 1303. Photograph: Paige Critcher.

**The Love of the 3 Oranges.** 1939-60.
Oil on canvas, 39 x 31 cm.
Martha Daura collection, 1432. Photograph: Paige Critcher.

**Baseball.** 1939-55.
Oil on cardboard, 38 x 27 cm.
Chrysler Museum of Art, Norfolk.

**Baseball.** 1939-55.
Oil on cardboard, 38 x 27 cm.
Chrysler Museum of Art, Norfolk.

**Baseball.** 1939-55.
Oil on cardboard, 38 x 27 cm.
Chrysler Museum of Art, Norfolk.

**St. John the Baptist.** 1953.
Wood, 101 x 22 x 14 cm.
Lynchburg College, Lynchburg.

**Adolescence.** 1945-53.
Paper pulp, 167 x 127 x 51 cm.
Martha Daura collection, 9025.  Photograph: Paige Critcher.

**André Breton.** 1955-60.
Wood, 30 x 37 x 3 cm.
Musée des Augustins, Toulouse.

**Mother and Child.** 1959.
Holly, 65 x 28 x 28 cm.
Martha Daura collection, 9018. Photograph: Paige Critcher.

**Pieta from Rubeo.** 1939-57.
Oil on cardboard, 36 x 28 cm.
Martha Daura collection, 1355. Photograph: Paige Critcher.

**Pieta.** ca. 1950.
Oil on cardboard, 32 x 22 cm.
Museu Diocesà de Menorca, Ciutadella. Photograph: Cisco Moll.

**The Family.** 1939-57.
Oil on cardboard, 76 x 61 cm.
Martha Daura collection, 1379.  Photograph: Paige Critcher.

**Remember Pearl Harbor.** 1942-45.
Gouache on cardboard, 55 x 78 cm.
Martha Daura collection, 1492. Photograph: Paige Critcher.

**Americans at Work.** 1942-45.
Gouache on cardboard, 99 x 64 cm.
Martha Daura collection, 1488. Photograph: Paige Critcher.

**Golden Glow.** ca. 1957.
Oil on canvas, 78 x 64 cm.
San Antonio Museum of Art.

# CHANGE OF STYLE: ST. CIRQ LAPOPIE

In the summer of 1947, Daura returned to St. Cirq after an absence of eight years. The medieval house had survived the war intact, but much of the furniture had disappeared; curiously enough, it began to reappear when the neighbors saw that Daura was back. The Dauras continued to spend their summer vacations in St. Cirq, and beginning with 1953, when Daura gave up his teaching job, they stayed there even longer.

After Martha graduated from Wellesley College, she joined the U.S. diplomatic service. In December 1952, she was given her first assignment: Paris. Martha made frequent trips to St. Cirq, and this gave Louise and Pierre another reason for making longer visits. Moreover, the contact with the medieval village, the cliffs, plateaus and valleys was vital to Daura. The experience it afforded — almost mystical — was what moved him to paint. "*In Saint Cirq... I was deliriously seeking — once more, just once more, so went my prayer — ecstasies, possession, transcendence or communion, just once more... with Beauty... my own one, because made out of the whole of my fragmented being.*"[96]

During the summer of 1955, Daura wrote to his sister-in-law, Betty Blair, from St. Cirq,[97] explaining how, in an old copy of *Time* magazine, a caption under a photograph of William Faulkner's old house had caught his eye. It read: "*Its master is at home, only at home.*" These words led Daura to reflect on his own life and home. Separation from his roots and frequent moves had caused him to lose the sense of place which all creators need, a foundation on which to base their work. For Daura, the caption became "*a drama deep, and dark, and infinite, and powerfully frightful. All in eight words, in twenty seven letters, seven intervals.*" Inspired by this sentence, Daura wrote a poem of fifty-four lines. It is an interesting reflection on the solitude and nostalgia produced by not having a home, a living space in which to grow and create.

"*And I wonder if that mansion, where time had remained still, was, to Faulkner Home... Home... home... home... Let*

**Daura in his St. Cirq studio.** 1950s.
Photograph: Mopy-Maurice Charbonnières. Daura Archives.

*me go, Let me go... Let me go... I want to go home... Home. It is getting frightfully dark around me. Here and everywhere.*

*Dark and cold, bare and oppressing, boundless and bone crushing; it hurts.*
*Frightful emptiness, terrifying nothingness, mercilessly closing.*
*Though invisible, I see it closing.*
*Coming faster, closer, quieter, darker.*
*Nobody around? No brotherly hand?*

*— I must, I have to break through.*
*Let me go. Let me go.*
*I want to go home.*
*Faulkner is at home, only at home.*

*But Faulkner has his home.*
    *If I could go home.*
        *Home.*
*Home? Why home? What is home?*
    *I keep calling home!*
*Why? What is home? Do I have a Home?*

*Where is this home, Where, yes, where?*
*Here or there, is it there, anywhere, the true thing from which that mirage is made, that mirage that in my distress I call 'My Home'?"*

It seemed to Daura that he had found the home and the roots he sought in St. Cirq, in its church and its medieval houses. Certain fragments of his poem illustrate the works he painted at that time, paintings which also meant a new style. Louise explained this to Betty, in a letter written in August of 1955, using Daura's own words: "*Perhaps people won't like it, but for me it was as if, suddenly, St. Cirq had come back to life and, taking me by the hand, in a joyous folly, we danced a spirited bourrée.*" Louise adds: "*He throws on colour with abandon, not caring how expensive the tubes are, and painting just as he wants to, without thinking what the others will say.*"[98]

"*The stone, the mortar, the tiles, the stained glass windows; jewels, gems, scintillant lights, that is the calm, serene, unchanged church, around which I wanted to weave my home.*

*One hundred ruby like flames*
*More brilliant than fire or blood*
*When the dew or the rain has washed the dust*
*And refreshed the fired earth color*
*On the ruby red tiles of the one hundred steep climbing roofs.*

*One of these winding, old Cahors wine colored patches was in my feverish, the fever that comes from my chest, the roof under which my feverish dream had directed me at the crossing where my heart and my eyes would cry:*
    *This is home.*

*But the master is at home only at home.*"

That summer of 1955 in St. Cirq saw a major change in Daura's work. He painted with a new freedom, bringing the village houses to life. The pencil drawing, visible beneath the brushstrokes of color, accentuates the age of the houses, which unashamedly display the cracks of their walls. The eye-like windows and the mouth-like doors become expressive; the red roof provides a hat for houses which thus become almost alive. With his black pencil, Daura created angles to contrast with a pure white. He drew the houses heavy with the weight of the centuries, but as though they were living and eager to tell the thousand and one stories which had unfolded before them in the streets. The St. Cirq landscapes, beginning with 1955, had less depth and volume than his earlier work, but they gained in expressiveness. They no longer sought a third dimensional quality, but accepted the flat surface of canvas and paper.

Daura explained this change by saying that he had suddenly understood the language spoken by the houses of St. Cirq: "*Little I thought then… while facing the glowing tower of the ageless church, and the tower and the sky spoke to me in their each one's tongue; tongue on a Rosetta stone that only possessed artists can decipher — such a beautiful tongue! Such rich, vivid language a man can't keep it for himself alone, and was trying, humbly but with all my fury (all that I had left, that is), to translate into forms and colors, what the roofs, what the sky, what the tower were telling me… How we chattered, the old companions and I. I had not painted them for so many years. We had not spoken to each other for so long. This time, we find each other, our passion for each other renewed, bursting exuberantly. So much to tell each other after so many years of silence. We had aged some little plenty, no doubt. But we understood each other so much better now.*"[99]

In St. Cirq he again met some of his Catalan friends who had remained in France. He kept in touch by letter with other friends who had gone further afield in exile, and with those who had returned to Catalonia.[100]

In the early fifties, Daura began a close friendship with one of his St. Cirq neighbors, the Surrealist poet André Breton. In September 1951, Breton sent Daura a book by Jean Louis Bedouin, *Poetes d'Aujourd'hui*, with a poem to Daura, handwritten by Breton on the title page:

"*Chaque matin*
*Le plaisir était de voir naître*
*De ma fenêtre*
*Une fumée bleue*

*Je me disais*
*Voici mon ami Pierre Daura qui se lève*

*Cette fumée*
*Voile et dévoile*

*Un comportement humain comme je les aime*
*Et comme j'en sais peu*

*Que tout été*
*Retrouve cette fumée bleue."*

St. Cirq la Popie, Sept. 1951
André Breton

From my window
Each morning
I rejoiced at seeing
The birth of a blue smoke.

I would say to myself
There, my friend Pierre Daura is up.

This smoke
Veils and unveils
A sensitive and compassionate nature such as I like
And find so few of.

May that blue smoke
Rise again each summer.

In their letters, they related how they were spending the winter months, and spoke of mutual friends, of their neighbors in St. Cirq, and often of art. They also wrote about interesting exhibitions they had seen, and about new magazines and books that had come out and which they often exchanged. In a letter to Daura of April 1954, Breton explained that he was working on his book *L'Art Magique*.[101]

That the two were born on the same day of the same year was of great astrological significance to Breton, and was a factor which brought the two artists even closer together. Daura, inspired by a poem by Breton, painted *Star Makers*, an abstract work dominated by its sky-blue color. It was one of the major works in the show Daura held in 1955, at the Lynchburg Art Center.[102] The exhibition, titled "Variations on a Familiar Theme", included works painted during the preceding summer at St. Cirq. There were works on a religious theme, such as *The Holy Family* and *The Prophet*, and a series of five variations on the theme of *Maternity*. Daura used his new painting technique of broken black lines contrasting with pure white, a style which a critic lost no time in comparing to that of El Greco.[103] The show included sculptures, and landscapes of his village of St. Cirq which had inspired his new style. The critics and the public were surprised by the change in Daura's art, by its renewed vitality and spontaneity, and some saw it as a "rebirth" of his work.[104]

The influence of Catalan Romanesque art is evident in Daura's religious work. The majesty and frontal representation of the figures, and the delineation of the colors with thick black lines, are all reminiscent of the frescoes which decorated the early churches in the Pyrenees.

In 1957, Daura had a solo show at the Roanoke Arts Center, featuring landscapes of St. Cirq and Rockbridge Baths, watercolors of variations on a still life theme, and some sculptures.[105] In the same year, he had a second exhibition at the Lynchburg Art Center.[106]

---

96. Letter from Daura to Ray Hamaker, author of the poem "Vision at the Tower of Saint Cirq", December 8, 1955, Daura Archives.

97. Letter from Daura to Betty Blair, June 7, 1955, Daura Archives.

98. *"Peut-être les gens ne l'aimeront pas, mais pour moi c'est comme si tout d'un coup Saint Cirq redevenu vivant m'aurait pris de par la main et dans une joie folle nous dansions une bourrée joyeuse."* Letter from Louise to Betty Blair, August 31, 1955, Daura Archives.

99. Letter from Daura to Ray Hamaker, op. cit.

100. Daura correspondence with Berenguel, Bosch-Roger, Cochet, Commeleran, Fernández, Jou, Senabre, Torres-García, and others, Daura Archives.

101. Letter from André Breton to Daura, April 22, 1954, Daura Archives.

102. "Daura One-man Show Opens at Art Center," *The News*, Lynchburg, December 5, 1955, p. 8; and "Spontaneity Marks Daura Works on Display at Lynchburg Center", *The Advance*, Lynchburg, December 5, 1955.

103. "At The Art Center", *The News*, Lynchburg, December 8, 1955.

104. *The News*, Lynchburg, December 8, 1955.

105. *An Exhibition of Works of Pierre Daura*, Roanoke Fine Arts Center, Roanoke, October 28-November 16, 1957.

106. *25th Civic Art Show*, Lynchburg Art Club, Lynchburg, November 10-17, 1957.

**Church. St. Cirq Lapopie.** ca. 1955.
Oil on canvas, 71 x 38 cm.
Martha Daura collection, 2313. Photograph: Benoit Petit.

**Chapel and Roofs.** St. Cirq Lapopie. ca. 1956.
Oil on canvas, 50 x 61 cm.
Museu Diocesà de Menorca, Ciutadella. Photograph: Cisco Moll.

**Returning from Church.** St. Cirq Lapopie. ca. 1958.
Oil on canvas, 63 x 81 cm.
Martha Daura collection, 1092. Photograph: Paige Critcher.

**Children Playing.** St. Cirq Lapopie. ca. 1958.
Oil on canvas, 61 x 71 cm.
Martha Daura collection, 1093.  Photograph: Paige Critcher.

**Church and Presbytery**. St. Cirq Lapopie. ca. 1955.
Oil on paper, 81 x 64 cm.
Martha Daura collection, 1077.  Photograph: Paige Critcher.

**Church and Presbytery.** St. Cirq Lapopie. ca. 1955.
Oil on canvas, 81 x 66 cm.
Martha Daura collection, 1087.  Photograph: Paige Critcher.

**The Church.** St. Cirq Lapopie. ca. 1955.
Oil on canvas, 81 x 61 cm.
Martha Daura collection, 1076. Photograph: Paige Critcher.

**Daura House.** St. Cirq Lapopie. ca. 1955.
Oil on canvas, 76 x 105 cm.
Martha Daura collection, 2318. Photograph: Benoit Petit.

**T**here **Was a River.** St. Cirq Lapopie. ca. 1958.
Oil on canvas, 71 x 61 cm.
Martha Daura collection, 1099. Photograph: Paige Critcher.

**Breton House and Lot**. St. Cirq Lapopie. ca. 1963.
Oil on canvas, 62 x 73 cm.
Martha Daura collection, 1097. Photograph: Paige Critcher.

**Self-portrait.** 1960-69.
Oil on canvas, 48 x 31 cm.
Martha Daura collection, 1253. Photograph: Paige Critcher.

# THE FINAL YEARS: ROCKBRIDGE BATHS

In 1959, the Dauras left the apartment in Lynchburg where they had lived since 1945, and moved into a new house in Rockbridge Baths, just a few steps from the Baths (the warm springs), near the Maury River, and in the foothills of the Allegheny Mountains. Once again in intimate contact with nature, Daura spent his days the way he preferred: painting the countryside.

In February 1959, Daura had a show at Hollins College in Roanoke. The exhibition included sculptures in stone, wood and paper pulp, still lifes from 1927, two figure studies of Argelès from 1939, but the show emphasized recent works on a religious theme and landscapes of St. Cirq.[107] In April 1959, Daura presented a selection of his latest work at the Lynchburg Art Center.[108] Daura was asked to write a short article explaining the meaning of the art in the exhibition, for the Art Center magazine, *TAM* (Theater-Art-Music). He wrote: "*One day, all of a sudden, I was struck by the thought of how important and magical was the gift to man, his power to see. To see from without and from within.... How that power to see was the force setting in motion man's mind. There and then I decided that, as one lights and offers reverently a candle of thanks at the Altar of Faith, so my paintings thereafter would try to be like an exalted hymn offering*

    *to the joy of seeing*
    *to the joy of existing*
    *to the magic of feeling.*
    *So... hence this exhibit to my friends.*"[109]

Daura had another one-man show in Lexington, in January 1961, at Washington & Lee University. It included work drawings of Corsica, oil and watercolor landscapes, sculptures — some geometric and others with religious themes — and some works from the Cercle et Carré period.[110] In March he had a solo exhibition in Blacksburg.[111]

In April 1962, Daura had a show at the Staunton Fine Arts Center. Horace Day, the head of the Art Department at Mary Baldwin College in Staunton, described Daura's style

**Daura**. 1960s.
Photograph: Robert Munger. Daura Archives.

as lyric expressionism, and compared his work to that of the Austrian expressionist, Oscar Kokoschka,[112] who, like Daura, had painted the horrors of war. Daura described the realism of his works: "*Realism means reaching beneath the factual shell of a subject and touching closely the personality, the mood, the meaning of importance.*"[113]

In 1963, Daura returned to the Lynchburg Fine Arts Center for another show, with oils, watercolors, drawings, sculp-

**Daura at home.** Rockbridge Baths. 1960s.
Photograph: Washington & Lee University.

tures and some engravings from his days in Paris. In 1967, he exhibited a selection of paintings and sculptures at Washington & Lee University, in Lexington.[114] The following year, Virginia Military Institute, in Lexington, organized a major exhibition of Daura's work, which was shown with that of another painter, Marion Junkin.[115]

In August 1969, the Maury River flooded the Daura house, damaging Daura's art which had been organized in piles on the floor, ready to be taken to three galleries for shows. Daura lost over two hundred watercolors and many oils and sculptures. In the summer of 1970, he took part in a group show in St. Cirq.[116] In 1973, Mary Baldwin College, in Staunton,[117] gave him a one-man show, and in 1974, it was Lynchburg College[118] which organized a major Daura exhibition, with over sixty works, ranging from an oil painting of the port of Barcelona done in 1908 to a recent sculpture.

During his last years in Virginia, Daura devoted himself entirely to the activity which gave him most satisfaction: creating. He painted every day, with oil or watercolor, and he sculpted. Until the last, he never lacked creative force, or the "gift of painting", which Torres-García had attributed to him as far back as 1928. Beginning with a subject, or a theme, such as a tree with autumn colors, a chicken house, or a platter of fruit, he enjoyed doing a series of watercolors, which developed from the figurative subject to an abstract synthesis of it. Sometimes the themes he chose were taken from paintings he had done much earlier. Landscapes of Corsica and Ibiza became the subjects of works in the late sixties. Daura found themes within himself as well as in the countryside around him. As his mobility lessened, he used that rich inner world of experiences and memories as inspiration for his painting. He was often overtaken by nostalgia, by recollections of his childhood, and of the country he would not live in again. When Louise died in 1972, his loneliness was even harder to bear.

The decision taken when he was young, to devote his life to art, was never questioned, though his priorities did change. At first he wanted to be a success, and to be part of the avant-garde. Then he became a teacher, to help people understand art, and in the last two decades of his life, he wished simply to communicate to others the joy he felt at being able to create. He chose an individual, solitary path, which did not, however, take him away from the considerations that moved mankind in the second half of the twentieth century.

Daura died in Lexington, Virginia, on January 1, 1976. After his death, several institutions in Virginia honored him with tributes and exhibitions: Virginia Military Institute, Lexington (1977), Lynchburg Fine Arts Center, Lynchburg (1978), and Virginia Polytechnic Institute and State University, Blacksburg (1979). In France, the Museum of Cahors had a retrospective in 1979. In September 1990, the Daura Gallery, an extension of the Dillard Fine Arts Center at Lynchburg College, was dedicated to Pierre and Louise. The

Daura archives are kept in a subsequent addition to the Daura Gallery, opened in 1995, and some of his works are permanently on view there. In Barcelona, in May 1977, two of his paintings were included in the exhibition "The Catalan Avant-garde. 1916 -1936": a still life from 1929, and a landscape from 1922.[119] It seems very appropriate that these two oils were shown beside the work of Pere Créixams, Josep Granyer, Gargallo, Juli González, Joan Miró, Joan Junyer, Joan Sandalinas, Josep de Togores and Joaquín Torres-García, most of them artists with whom Daura had close ties in his youth.

Towards the end of his life, Daura did an extraordinary series of self-portraits in which we see — as in the houses of St. Cirq — how the passing years weighed on the artist. These are done with confident, flowing brushstrokes, and sometimes the painter is surrounded by a warm golden light. Perhaps this light is a sign that he faced old age with the serenity of having done what he set out to do, and of having remained true to his principles. Daura left a body of work which was coherent and consistent with his chosen life, and which reflected what had concerned him so much since he was a young man: the truth, his truth.

107. "Hollins to Exhibit Art Works by Daura", *The News*, Lynchburg, February 1, 1959.

108. *Pierre Daura*, Lynchburg Art Center, Lynchburg, April 19-May 1, 1959.

109. Letter from Louise to her family, April 29 1959, Daura Archives.

110. Priscilla Young: "Pierre Daura and To Man, Compassion", *The Roanoke Times,* Roanoke, January 8, 1961; and Robert S. Munger: "Daura Exhibition Proves Artist's Strength, Versatility", *Rockbridge County News*, Lexington, January 12, 1961.

111. *Art Festival*, Blacksburg Art Association, Blacksburg, March 26-31, 1961.

112. Gracious Galbraith: "One-man Show at Staunton Fine Arts Center a Success", *Staunton News Leader*, Staunton, April 22, 1962; "International Artist to Exhibit at Center Here", *Staunton News Leader,* Staunton, April 8, 1962.

113. Priscilla Young: "Pierre Daura's Work on Display", *The Roanoke Times,* Roanoke, October 28, 1962.

114. *Pierre Daura, An Exhibition of Painting and Sculpture*, duPont Gallery, Washington & Lee University, Lexington, April 6-30, 1967.

115. *Pierre Daura & Marion Junkin*, Lejeune Hall, Virginia Military Institute, Lexington, April 1-19, 1968.

116. *IIème Exposition de l'Eté 70, Hommage de Groupe a St. Cirq Lapopie*, Musée J. Rignault, St. Cirq Lapopie, August, 1970.

117. *Pierre Daura, Paintings, Watercolors & Sculptures*, Mary Baldwin College, Staunton, October 29 to November 17, 1973.

118. "Mr. Daura. An Exhibition of His Works", Dillard Fine Arts Building, Lynchburg College, Lynchburg, 1974; *The News*, Lynchburg, November 24, 1974.

119. The 1929 work, done near the Cercle et Carré period, appears to be incorrectly dated 1921 in the catalogue *Avantguarda catalana. 1916-1936*, Galeria Dau al Set, Barcelona, May 1977.

**Autumn.** Rockbridge Baths. 1951-71.
Oil on canvas, 66 x 81 cm.
Martha Daura collection, 1047.  Photograph: Paige Critcher.

**Feeding the Chickens.** Rockbridge Baths. ca. 1962.
Oil on canvas, 63 x 76 cm.
Martha Daura collection, 1057. Photograph: Paige Critcher.

**Autumn Fields**. Rockbridge Baths. 1955-70.
Watercolor on paper, 38 x 56 cm.
Martha Daura collection, 4566.  Photograph: Paige Critcher.

**The Kiln House.** Rockbridge Baths. 1955-70.
Watercolor on paper, 56 x 38 cm.
Asheville Museum of Art, NC.  Photograph: Paige Critcher.

**Self-portrait.** 1960-67.
Oil on cardboard, 61 x 45 cm.
Martha Daura collection, 1188. Photograph: Paige Critcher.

**Self-portrait.** 1960-69.
Oil on canvas, 61 x 49 cm.
Martha Daura collection, 1251. Photograph: Paige Critcher.

**Self-portrait.** ca. 1965.
Oil on canvas, 51 x 44 cm.
Martha Daura collection, 1231. Photograph: Paige Critcher.

**Self-portrait.** 1960-67.
Oil on canvas, 61 x 51 cm.
Martha Daura collection, 1190. Photograph: Paige Critcher.

**Self-portrait.** 1960-69.
Oil on cardboard, 81 x 38 cm.
Martha Daura collection, 1233. Photograph: Paige Critcher.

**Self-portrait.** 1960-69.
Oil on canvas, 51 x 38 cm.
Martha Daura collection, 1238. Photograph: Paige Critcher.

**Self-portrait.** 1970-71.
Oil on canvas, 61 x 51 cm.
Martha Daura collection, 1263. Photograph: Paige Critcher.

# PIERRE DAURA IN CATALAN ART: THE GENERATION OF 1917

Francesc Fontbona

We have read the biography of Pierre Daura. Now we should place him in his artistic context. Daura was undoubtedly a Catalan painter, by birth and by inclination; but life's circumstances led him to live abroad for many years, in France and in the United States, where he died. This means that although we can study his work and his career in an international context, we can see that Daura played a role in the evolution of Catalan art, which was then being enriched by external influences worth examining in order to complete the portrait we have of Daura.

The period in which Daura came to public attention was strongly marked by *Noucentisme* in Catalan art. I refer here to his first appearances as an established painter, for we must regard the exhibitions he organized with his fellow students between 1911 and 1913 as little more than anecdotes of adolescence.

*Noucentisme* was a cultural movement which enjoyed fleeting success: from the moment when it really burst upon the scene in 1911, until it began to be questioned in the country's leading intellectual circles, barely six years had passed. These were the halcyon years of the politics of Enric Prat de la Riba, the years of the gestation and initial activity of the *Mancomunitat de Catalunya* (the Regional Catalan Government) of which he was the President, a time when to many it seemed as though everything was either perfect or possible. These were the years when a classical esthetic was taking shape in Catalonia, exalting the myth of the Mediterranean. Rather than following the museum-like coldness of neo-classicism, it adopted canons with a warm, judiciously vibrant approach. This was certainly also due to Parisian influences on the development of modern art, mitigating the severity of classicism and leading to a hybrid, independent, alternative movement, distinct from its influences. *Noucentisme* was, then, an artistic current which brought together classicism and modernity, it was a cultural "product" which, despite its classical foundations, could not have emerged at any previous moment of history.

If Prat de la Riba's politics provoked a degree of discontent, the art of the period provoked dissent only in insignificant, conservative quarters. There was some controversy with Torres-García, but in his case it was due more perhaps to personal than to purely artistic factors. In the country at large, there was a general consensus that *Noucentisme* at its height would be the style of the period. Yet this consensus was frail and lasted just six years, when the spell of *Noucentisme* was violently broken. After a series of political events paved the way, a new generation of painters and sculptors introduced a considerable degree of dissidence into a hitherto almost idyllic setting. *Noucentisme* did not, however, end with this. It lingered for many years, but it gradually lost the status that it had enjoyed at its peak as the indisputable esthetic banner of an epoch.

The painters and sculptors who dethroned *Noucentisme* were the young artists of Daura's generation, the generation of 1917, newcomers to the artistic arena. Rather than an organized, coherent block, this generation consisted of four or five little groups, and various individuals. It was as though these young Catalan artists felt a special need to take the helm and change the course of the country's art, after the phase of peaceful idealism represented by *Noucentisme*.[1] The consensus of that movement had not lasted long, and once a few had hinted at change, many others were quick to follow. Perhaps if the leadership of Prat de la Riba had continued, *Noucentisme* would have remained unscathed for a longer time, but that is only a possibility, and possibilities are a poor working basis for history. The fact is that Prat, who was the keystone of a political and cultural edifice, died in 1917, the year in which so many things changed in Catalonia.

However, the young artists of the generation of 1917 did not simply want to leave *Noucentisme* behind. They were also reacting against the brilliant, superficial colorism of the more popular, less intellectual, more "Spanish" art shows, which, although numerous, have tended to be virtually ignored by Catalan art historians. Although the critics did not pay much attention to this rather commercial form of painting, so very different from *Noucentisme*, it had a considerable popular appeal in the street, which gave another reason for it to be rejected by these young malcontents who wanted to purify Catalan art.

The first two groups of young artists of the generation to burst upon the Catalan art scene with changes were the Evolutionists and the Agrupació Courbet (Courbet Group). From the beginning, the Courbet Group paid its respects to *Noucentisme*, probably because many of its members were disciples of Francesc d'A. Galí, the art teacher who was most identified with the group. In 1915, the future members of the Courbet Group (which did not yet officially exist) published a review which sought to challenge the cultural awareness of Vilanova, the town where most of them lived. This publication bore a name typical of *Noucentisme*: "Themis."

The initial core of the group was formed by Enric-C. Ricart, Rafael Sala and Joan Miró, and its sponsor or godfather, a man of many talents — poet, draftsman and critic — came from outside the group: Josep Maria Junoy. By early 1918, we can say that the Courbet Group officially existed. It was soon joined by Francesc Domingo and by Josep Llorens i Artigas, an art critic who was appointed the group manager, and who would later be recognized in art history as one of the most prestigious ceramists of Europe.[2]

It was in February-March 1918 that Miró had his first solo exhibition at the Galeries Dalmau, which was the platform from which one after another emerging Catalan artist launched his career. Josep F. Ràfols and Marian A. Espinal soon joined the Courbet Group, which, under the auspices of the Cercle Artístic de Sant Lluc, participated in a show held in Barcelona in the spring of 1918. In December of the same year, the group took part, under its name, in the first autumn salon organized by the interesting but short-lived Associació d'Amics de les Arts.

The Courbet Group soon enlarged its ranks with the addition of Joaquín Torres-García, Rafael Benet, Josep Obiols and Josep de Togores, although only Benet became fully integrated. Torres-García was undergoing a moment of crisis after breaking with the Regional Government of Puig i Cadafalch, and the only thing he was really sure of was his desire to leave the country. The group stayed the course through 1919, when it held a show in May at the Galeries Laietanes.[3] By 1920, in spite of the ties between individuals, many members had drifted away.

The esthetic position of the Courbet Group was clearly similar in approach to Fauvism. There were unmistakable roots in *Noucentisme* and a strong Cézannesque tendency. This was modified by a degree of deliberate naiveté, omnipresent in European art since Paul Gauguin had spectacularly called for art to return to its origins, to primitivism, as a source of all artistic renewal. The fact that some group members, like Joan Miró, blazed their own avant-garde trails with high international profiles illustrates the innovative ambition of the group's approach, but is not proof of an overall esthetic relationship on the part of the "Courbets". They were, in general, innovative, or "modern", but not iconoclastic.

The Evolutionists, fired by the same spirit of renewal as the Courbets, came from a different background, and had a harder approach. While the members of the Courbet Group generally came from the most purist, modern Catalan artistic circles, the somewhat rebellious younger brothers of the representatives of *Noucentisme*, the Evolutionists tended to be snipers who patrolled District V (a poor Barcelona district). As one of them, the sculptor Josep Granyer, recalled, they were "guttersnipes" and the others were "nice young men".[4] For this reason, the Courbets joined the group exhibition circuit in Barcelona sooner than the Evolutionists.

The Evolutionists organized in 1917, the year in which a series of political, social and cultural events changed the premises of some young Catalan artists. In May they announced their existence as a group, though not yet under what was to be their *nom de guerre*. The setting was an end-of-course show by students of the municipal school in District V, where they had studied under Francesc Labarta. The show purported to be a manifesto of the new form of art teaching preached by Labarta, and it was hailed as such by Francesc Pujols.[5] Labarta sought to awaken in the student the ability to abstract the qualities of the model, from the general to the particular and, in the process, to do away with the differences "between official teaching and modern artistic production". The result was a forceful show dominated by a schematic representation of Cézannesque volumes, which undoubtedly was the point of departure for that group of artists who, while mindful of the guidance of their teacher, would try out their own wings.

As Evolutionists, their theory — and the group's name — was taken from the *Art-Evolution* manifesto published in September 1917 by Joaquín Torres-García, a prestigious and charismatic artist who was adopting avant-garde positions,[6] and who in his subsequent Parisian period was to belong to Cercle et Carré as did Daura, as Teresa Macià has already explained.

The Evolutionists were: Joan Cortés, more a theoretician than a practicioner, but author of a small yet interesting body of work;[7] Alfred Sisquella; Joan Serra; Ernest Enguiu; Francesc Elias; Eduard Vergez, who in February 1918 had had a one-man show at the Galeries Dalmau; Antoni Canadell; and the sculptor Josep Viladomat. They exhibited as a group at the Galeries Dalmau in March 1918.

Independently of their artistic style, the Evolutionists projected a rather disturbing personal image; Sebastià Gasch recalls how they would saunter down the boulevard of La Rambla "at a weary pace and with a challenging air, attracting the attention of passers-by because of their untidiness, which could be seen as a gesture of independence and rebellion with, perhaps, the added convenience of doing away with the irksome dictates of hygiene and the complex tyrannies of coquetry".[8] Their desire to counteract idealism and bright colors led them to paint in "neutral, dark tones",[9] a characteristic which Feliu Elias explained in the following words: "once again we will insist on the neutral palette" — he had previously said "dirty and earthy" — "which, as though by contagion, this small community of painters cultivates. We wish to make it understood that we do not censure this toning down and dirtying of colors, for although the opposite vice — easier and more plebeian — of making pure colors sing stridently is always preferable, we have to admit that the good tone and the intention of the muted harmonies in many of these works do express what the painter wished to say."[10]

In April, a month after the March 1918 Dalmau show, a group exhibition at the same gallery brought together the Evolutionists and the Courbets, who shared the space with Barradas, Torres-García and Pere Ysern Alié. It was not a major exhibition, as it was a collection of works by artists associated with the gallery,[11] but it did serve to bring together the two foremost groups of young artists and two of the most avant-garde painters then working in Catalonia, Barradas and Torres-García.

The initiative taken by the Courbets and the Evolutionists encouraged the appearance of other groups of young artists with similar interests. These were the Agrupació d'Artistes Catalans (Group of Catalan Artists) and the Saló Nou Ambient, which also had their first exhibitions at the Galeries Dalmau, the most radically innovative art venue of the time, in two group shows which took place in February and March 1919.

Daura formed part of the Group of Catalan Artists, and participated in the group exhibition along with Emili Bosch-

Roger, Pere Farró, Josep Girbau, Ferran Mussons, Miquel Muntané, Josep Salvà, Agapit Vidal Salichs, Francesc Vidal Gomà and Jaume Vila.

Daura came to the world of art simply and naturally: he started painting as a child "knowing neither why nor how".[12] As we have seen in the main chapter of this book, he studied art under José Ruiz, Pablo Picasso's father, and Josep Calvo, the venerable teacher of set design. This was a specialty in which Daura became especially involved, because he worked with a set designer to earn his living. He also went to the popular night classes at schools in the Carrer del Carme and Carrer Tallers, he read, and he traveled. He was guided by the painter and teacher Antoni Gelabert i Alart (who also taught many members of the Saló Nou Ambient) and, above all, by a prestigious character of the period in popular, enlightened left-wing circles, the respected patriarch, Eudald Canibell.[13]

When Daura joined the Group of Catalan Artists, he had scarcely experienced the artistic atmosphere of Barcelona, for he had spent several years in Paris,[14] and he was shortly to spend three years in Minorca for his compulsory military service, after which, in 1920, he returned to the French capital.

In Paris, Daura learned woodcut engraving from his Catalan friend, Lluís Jou, who had been a dedicated follower of Canibell, and who was a successful wood engraver and publisher of collectors' books in France.[15] However, his links with the artistic life of Catalonia were primarily with the Group of Catalan Artists, and although he was unable to participate in the exhibition of January 1920, he did take part in those of February 1922 and January 1925, both held, as usual, at the Galeries Dalmau. In February 1927, the group held another show, but this time at the Sala Parés.[16]

Many years later, when he was living in the U.S., Daura still kept in touch with the friends of his youth, such as Bosch-Roger (who always kept a good Daura oil painting), Commeleran and Granyer.[17] As he said of the old Catalan artists of his generation: "...the friends who remain remember me. And I remember them."[18]

Of all the groups of young artists which emerged in those years, the shortest-lived was the Courbet Group, paradoxically the one which subsequently received the most publicity. However, the Group of Catalan Artists went on, as we have seen, to hold shows in 1920 and 1922, while the Saló Nou Ambient — even more active, and including, among others, Camps-Ribera, Alfons Iglésias, Ramon Soler Liró, Francesc Vidal-Galícia and Antoni Roca — held exhibitions in 1920, 1921, 1922 and 1923, in addition to the exhibition held in homage to Nonell in 1922. As well as these shows at the Galeries Dalmau, we should mention the second Saló de Tardor, organized in late 1920 by the Associació d'Amics de les Arts, which the Saló Nou Ambient and the Evolutionists attended in bloc.

The longevity of the Saló Nou Ambient was due in great part to the review it created with the same name. Six issues of *Nou Ambient* were published in 1924. The group exhibited in 1924 and 1925, the second time at Barcelona's Sala Camarín. The group had practically dissolved, and associated more and more with members of the Group of Catalan Artists, when it had its last exhibition in 1932, at the Galeria Les Arts, in Barcelona.[19]

Other groups were to emerge, such as the Saló Noucentista, when it seemed as though this name had outlived its capacity for expression. Founded in 1921 by Alfred Figueras, Rafael Tona and others, it too was short-lived. In May 1922, this group exhibited at the Galeries Dalmau, but curiously, without either Figueras — who was doing his military service — or Tona.

It was the Evolutionists, apparently not yet consolidated as a group, who were to become, albeit only nominally, the successors of their fellow groups. In 1923 they took part in a Barcelona exhibition under the Evolutionists name, with the addition of the painters Josep Mompou and Julián Castedo, and the sculptors Josep Granyer and Joan Rebull. In May 1924 and May 1925 they held further group shows at the Galeries Dalmau, when the group was joined by Ramon de Capmany.

In February 1931, there was a kind of resurrection of the Evolutionists at the Sala Parés, and in April 1932 — the year of the swan song of Nou Ambient — they had a further exhibition in Madrid, organized by Maragall of the Sala Parés. This was the last effort of the group, which by then was leading a rather forced existence, although it did bring together artists with tendencies similar to those of the group, but who had not been in it at its peak.

So there was an entire generation of young Catalan painters, members of specific groups or more or less on their own, who formed a solid, homogeneous block despite their individual diversity, and who dominated some twenty years of Catalan painting. Although Daura worked at a distance from these painters, he was always close to them in spirit. His frequent physical distance encouraged a degree of independence, which he described in these words: "every day you think, live, paint differently; this is the price of solitude. What a deep pit curiosity is. Naturally enough, the result is

that no one knows x the painter. Because perhaps in his never-ending research, x the painter has never actually existed. It may be pretentious, but I think that I could be like x the painter. And there are so many in Catalonia, in Spain...."[20]

Except for three years of military service in Minorca from 1917 to 1920, Daura lived in Paris from 1914 to 1930, when, having married the Virginia painter Louise Blair, he moved to St. Cirq Lapopie, in Aquitaine. It was during his last two years in Paris that he was one of the three founders of the major French abstract art group, Cercle et Carré, but this did not stop him from painting in Catalonia — Altafulla (1929), Montserrat (1931) — and Majorca (1932), and from taking part in Catalan exhibitions. He had one-man shows in Barcelona, at the Sala Badrinas (May 1929) and at the Galeria Syra (November-December 1932). The first featured landscapes of Corsica and Catalonia — Altafulla, La Fatarella and Ascó — as well as still lifes; and the second included paintings, drawings and watercolors, of Altafulla, Montserrat, Majorca and St. Cirq.

His group shows included the exhibition of National and Foreign Modern Art, organized by the Galeries Dalmau in November 1929, where Daura presented an excellent Modiglianesque portrait of his wife, now at the Musée Hyacinthe Rigaud in Perpignan,[21] and the exhibition of the competition "Montserrat vist pels pintors catalans" (Montserrat as seen by Catalan artists), from December 1931 to the following February, in which he entered two views of the Path to the Cave (morning and afternoon) and one of the Path of St. Michael. The latter was awarded one of the first prizes, the St. Cecilia prize.

At the famous Exposició del Nu (Exhibition of Nudes) in Barcelona of December 1933, Daura's painting caused a scandal, adding to the indignation already voiced by Catalan puritans over the subject of the exhibition. One of their number, the writer Ramon Rucabado, wrote: "'filth', and more than filth, the worst kind of filth, is the only term to be applied to Pere Daura's nude."[22] The nude in question, a woman reclining on a cushion, is now at the Musée Hyacinthe Rigaud, in Perpignan, and despite showing the nude body with no concern for concealment, there is absolutely nothing provocative about it to justify Rucabado's broadside.[23] In the same month, Daura had a one-man show in Barcelona, once again at the Galeries Syra. He showed still lifes, some of flowers, figures, compositions and landscapes of St. Cirq and a place titled "La Chartreuse". Although he was living in France, Daura was still very much part of the artistic life of Catalonia.

Daura kept his ties to Catalonia, and the review *Art* (one of the few publications which symbolize an era and validate everything they discuss) devoted a well illustrated article to him.[24] At a time when the trend begun by the painters of the generation of 1917 had become almost the official art of Catalonia (the Catalonia of the Republican Government), Daura, one of the founding members of that movement, was reaping his fair share of their collective success.

He was still to hold another one-man show in Barcelona, in December 1935, at the Sala Barcino, this time with land-scapes of Virginia. In the midst of the Spanish Civil War, in 1937, Joan Merli, the former editor of *Art*, wrote the book *33 pintors catalans* (33 Catalan painters), published by the information division of the Generalitat de Catalunya (Catalan Government), and one of the thirty-three was Daura. This book recognized Daura as one of the definitive artists of his time in Catalonia, despite his living in France — there was no distance in 1937, as the painter was fighting the war here in Catalonia — and despite his "independent spirit, rebelling against any kind of repressive law, refusing to sit on the fence", as Merli described him.[25]

With the end of the Spanish Civil War, the Catalan Daura came to an end, as did the restless, driven Daura. Nonetheless, when the first Saló d'Octubre was held in Barcelona, in 1948, the young organizers — the future leaders of a new Catalan avant-garde — opened the show with a special room paying homage to eight great artists, including the distant Daura.[26] But one flower does not make a summer.

The American Daura was now a long way away, and his career ambitions were muted. In justifying his too critical assessment of his mature period (in a letter written when Louise was dying and he was three years from death, in a Catalan rusty from lack of use), he said: "the reason I perhaps did not speak more about my esthetic evolution after the war is that this evolution never really had body, or place, or direction, or valor, or intensity."[27] For him, "certainties, firm, absolute definitions" were very important to artistic creation. However, he added, "and as those certainties have not come to me, or have always been short-lived, … dear friend, I am still searching".[28] Truly, this was a very hard confession and, without a doubt, most unjust, for if his work in the long postwar years did not fully reflect his earlier ambition to break new ground, it was still beautiful painting, the result of the wisdom of many years of living art.

Although Daura had no place in the history of contemporary Catalan art, he was conscious of the value of his art. According to Torres-García, who was a very close friend, "he

was humble in his pride, in his moral integrity, but always proud, without seeming it".[29]

Daura was one of the leading figures of that generation of 1917, which awakened a new manner of poetizing figuration. Many of his companions of that generation (Bosch-Roger, Mompou, Joan Serra, Sisquella, Benet, Capmany), after breaking, often violently, with various Catalan painting traditions, paradoxically ended up being identified by the avant-garde with another form of traditionalism, simply because they based their art on external reality and form. Daura was not relegated to the same supposedly outmoded bag, simply because he was living in another country and had been forgotten by many.

For the same reason, he was not considered when the new myths of the avant-garde were being created, despite the fact that, in Paris, he was one of the major names of the Cercle et Carré group, the bastion of international geometric abstraction.[30] He was only an integral part of the group for a short time, probably because its discipline was not in keeping with his character, in either artistic or human terms. Daura was basically an independent painter because he chose not to join any of the many institutionalized trends which make up the contemporary world art scene.

He was the creator of a body of work which, despite not bowing to modish tendency, still managed to carve out its own niche in the international context of Fauvism, a scenario followed to varying degrees by other European painters with relatively high-profile work. We tend to forget that the paths of expression forged by creativity are only really *viable* if they can be used, turned to good advantage and developed rather than continually disrupted in a kind of sterile ongoing revolution. Daura only disrupted what was strictly necessary; he was an artist who was stimulated by the world around him: the landscape, human form, natural elements. Rather than being one-sided, his interpretation of it often took the form of robust expressionism, set off at times by the purest lyricism, which made him a creator of a broad register of forms and a sensitive communicator of sensations. Rafael Benet, a leading authority on twentieth-century world painting — as well as being a member of the generation of 1917 — judiciously includes Daura among what he calls the *estilistes ponderats*, or "reflective stylists".[31]

For his style, and for his personal links with the most celebrated focal points of contemporary world art, Daura undoubtedly has a place — a foremost place — in the great arena occupied by other free, independent figurative artists of the École de Paris and its milieu who form roughly part of the same generation, such as Kars, Dunoyer de Segonzac, Krémegne, Kisling, Gromaire, Soutine, Caillard and Brianchon. They are all different, but all are linked by the same methodology: painting from real models, interpreted in the light of their knowledge of the totality of twentieth-century modernity.

Yet the space accorded to Daura in international art publications has not been equal to his merits. But time often heals wounds, and now, with this monograph and the rich new presence of Daura's work in our museums — and those of various other countries — the importance of this great painter who worked quietly in the wings can make itself felt, and, theory apart, his work will become a source of visual pleasure for the many people who are only now discovering it.

1 I write in more detail about the new direction taken by Catalan art after a series of events which took place in 1917 in Francesc Fontbona: *El paisatgisme a Catalunya*, Destino, Barcelona, 1979, pp. 269-309. For a systematic overview of the groups formed at this moment of crisis, see Francesc Miralles: "L'època de les avantguardes 1917-1970", vol. VIII of *Història de l'art català*, Edicions 62, Barcelona, 1983, pp. 21-30.

2 Llorens Artigas' membership was only partial: sometimes he appeared as a kind of spokesman for the group, but he never actually identified himself with the Agrupació Courbet, and in some of his reviews he was even harshly critical of the group's show. The formation of the group is described by an early witness, and one who was also to become a member, Josep F. Ràfols: *E. C. Ricart*, el cep i la nansa edicions, Vilanova i la Geltrú, 1981, p. 101 onwards.

3 The exhibition's invitation card featured Benet, Domingo, Espinal, Miró, Obiols, Ràfols, Ricart, Sala, Togores and Torres-García. By way of homage, Manolo, Humbert, Nogués, Picasso and Sunyer, all artists admired by the Courbets, headed the show.

4 Santos Torroella: "El 'Noucentisme' y los años veinte", *El Noticiero Universal*, Barcelona, November 5, 1974, p. 17.

5 Francesc Pujols: "Nova escola de dibuix", *Vell i Nou*, Barcelona, No. 44, June 1, 1917.

6 The fact that Torres-García ended up momentarily linked to the Agrupació Courbet instead of to the Evolutionists merely indicates that, apart from their respective inner circles, these groups, rather than being stable, self-contained bodies, were the expression of a general concern among the younger ranks of Catalan artists, which was manifested in a spontaneous, non-totalitarian fashion. Furthermore, one of the first — and highly favorable — reviews the Evolutionists had was signed by the Courbet member Josep Llorens i Artigas.

7 Cortés was also the group's best chronicler, with an article in the journal *Destino* (December 5, 1956), later included in Joan Cortès i Vidal: *Setanta anys de vida artística barcelonina*, Selecta, Barcelona, 1980, pp. 119-124.

8 Sebastián Gasch: "José Mompou en el recuerdo", *Destino*, Barcelona, July 27, 1968.

9 J. Ll[orens] i A[rtigas]: "Saló dels Evolucionistes", *La Veu de Catalunya*, Barcelona, March 25, 1918.

10 J. Sacs [Feliu Elias]: "En las Galerías Dalmau. Saló dels Evolucionistes", *La Publicidad*, Barcelona, March 13, 1918.

11 Torres-García and Barradas had already held a joint show at the Galeries Dalmau the previous December which did achieve a high profile.

12 Letter from Daura to Francesc Fontbona, February 18, 1972. Author's archives. My correspondence with the painter followed a query I sent when I was writing the article about him for the *Gran Enciclopèdia Catalana*.

13 All of this information comes from the same letter, which is partly autobiographical.

14 Daura (*ibid.*) writes: "In 1914, definitive trip to Paris. I was there to stay. Return to Spain 1918." It is strange that he stayed in France precisely during the years of World War I, which was when everyone else was leaving.

15 This is explained in a letter from Daura to Francesc Fontbona, March 6, 1972. Author's archives.

16 As Miralles points out, *op. cit.*, p. 30, this exhibition was subject to some censure from the critic Sebastià Gasch, due to the realist line it pursued at a time when some Catalan artists were at the center of a fundamental avant-garde venture at international level.

17 *Ibid.*

18 Letter from Daura to Francesc Fontbona, May 16, 1974. Author's archives.

19 See J. M. Cadena: "Nou Ambient', un grupo artístico y su revista", *Diario de Barcelona*, October 1, 1972, p. 13.

20 Letter from Daura to Francesc Fontbona, February 18, 1972.

21 Where it is exhibited with the title *Louise au béret rouge*.

22 R. Rucabado: *Bandera d'escàndol*, Políglota, Barcelona 1934, p. 83.

23 Marie-Claude Valaison: *Daura au Musée Hyacinthe Rigaud*, Perpignan, 1997, No. 44, pp. 23 and 42.

24 Joan Mates: "Pere Daura a Saint-Cirq", *Art*, Barcelona, No. 6, March 1934, pp. 177-182.

25 Joan Merli: *33 pintors catalans*, Comissariat de Propaganda de la Generalitat de Catalunya, Barcelona 1937, p. 63.

26 The other artists to be paid homage were Benet, Bosch-Roger, Domingo, Gausachs, Granyer, Humbert and Mercadé.

27 Letter from Daura to Francesc Fontbona, March 6, 1972.

28 *Ibid.*

29 Joaquín Torres-García: *Historia de mi vida*, Paidós, Barcelona - Buenos Aires - Mexico 1990, p. 184. (1st edition, Montevideo, 1939).

30 As Teresa Macià explains, Daura designed the group's emblem, used to head its printed material.

31 Rafael Benet: *Historia de la pintura moderna. Simbolismo*. Omega, Barcelona, 1953, p. 170.

EXHIBITIONS LIST

| 1911 | Barcelona | Estudi Vert | | P. Daura, E. Bosch-Roger, A. Vidal Salichs |
|------|-----------|-------------|---|---------------------------------------------|
| 1912 | Barcelona | Estudi Vert | | P. Daura, E. Bosch-Roger, A. Vidal Salichs |
| 1919 | Barcelona | Galeries Dalmau | | Agrupació d'Artistes Catalans |
| 1922 | Barcelona | Galeries Dalmau | | Agrupació d'Artistes Catalans |
| | Paris | | | Salon d'Automne |
| 1925 | Barcelona | Galeries Dalmau | | Agrupació d'Artistes Catalans |
| 1926 | Paris | | | Salon d'Automne |
| 1927 | Barcelona | Sala Parés | | Agrupació d'Artistes Catalans |
| | Paris | Galerie René Zivy | | Peinture Moderne |
| | Paris | La Sélection | | Peinture Moderne |
| 1928 | Paris | Galerie Marck | | Les Cinq Refusés |
| | Paris* | Galerie René Zivy | | Pierre Daura |
| 1929 | Barcelona | Galeries Dalmau | | Arte Moderno, Nacional y Extranjero |
| | Barcelona* | Sala Badrinas | | Paisatges de Còrsega |
| | Paris | Porte de Versailles | | Les Surindépendants |
| 1930 | Paris | Galerie 23 | | Cercle et Carré |
| | Barcelona | Galeries Laietanes | | Col·lecció Ferran Benet |
| | The Hague | | | Exposicions Selectes d'Art Contemporain |
| | Amsterdam | | | Exposicions Selectes d'Art Contemporain |
| 1931 | Paris | Galerie Billiet | | Peinture et Sculpture Catalane |
| | Montserrat | Monestir de Montserrat | | Montserrat vist pels artistes |
| | Barcelona | Palau Arts Decoratives | | Montserrat vist pels artistes |
| | Barcelona | Sala Badrinas | | Col·lectiva de pintura i escultura |
| 1932 | Barcelona | Palau Nacional | | Exposició de Primavera. Saló de Montjuïc |
| | Barcelona | Galeries Syra | | Fira del Dibuix |
| | Rosario, Arg.* | Signo Club. Salon Perla | | Pere Daura |
| | Cahors* | Musée de Cahors | | Pierre Daura |
| | Barcelona | Galeries d'Art Syra | | Artistes catalans contemporanis |
| | Barcelona* | Galeries d'Art Syra | | Obres de P. Daura 1915-1932 |
| 1933 | Amsterdam | Galerie d'Art A.Vecht | | Art Moderne Catalan |
| | Barcelona | Palau Nacional | | Exposició de Primavera. Saló de Montjuïc |
| | Figeac | Musée de Figeac | | Expositions de Beaux Arts et du Livre |
| | Barcelona* | Galeries d'Art Syra | | Pere Daura |
| | Barcelona | Cercle Artístic | | Exposició del Nu |
| | Lyon | Foire de Lyon | | Art Moderne Espagnol |
| | Barcelona | Sala Badrinas | | |
| 1934 | Barcelona | Palau Nacional | | Exposició de Primavera |
| | Toulouse | Chappe et Fils | | |
| 1935 | Tarrytown, NY | Westchester Institute of Fine Arts | | Annual Exhibition |
| | Barcelona* | Sala Barcino | | Pere Daura. Paisatges de Virgínia |
| 1936 | Buenos Aires, Arg. | | | Pintura Catalana |

| | | | |
|---|---|---|---|
| 1938 | Barcelona | | Saló de Tardor |
| 1940 | Hopewell, VA* | Woman's Club | Pierre Daura |
| 1941 | New Haven, CN | Yale University | |
| | Lynchburg, VA | Millner's | National Art Week |
| | Lynchburg, VA* | Lynchburg Art Gallery | Pierre Daura |
| 1942 | Richmond, VA | Virginia Museum of Fine Arts | Hélion & Daura |
| 1944 | Richmond, VA | Virginia Museum of Fine Arts | Watercolors by Virginia Artists |
| 1945 | Richmond, VA | Virginia Museum of Fine Arts | Watercolors by Virginia Artists |
| | Philadelphia, PA | Pennsylvania Academy of Fine Arts | Watercolors and Prints |
| | Philadelphia, PA* | Print Club Gallery | Pierre Daura |
| 1946 | Richmond, VA | Virginia Museum of Fine Arts | Watercolors by Virginia Artists |
| 1947 | Philadelphia, PA | Pennsylvania Academy of Fine Arts | Watercolors and Prints |
| 1948 | Richmond, VA | Virginia Museum of Fine Arts | Watercolors by Virginia Artists |
| | Barcelona | Galerias Layetanas | Salón de Octubre |
| 1949 | Richmond, VA | Virginia Museum of Fine Arts | Watercolors by Virginia Artists |
| 1950 | Lynchburg, VA | Randolph-Macon Art Gallery | Contemporary American Painting & Sculpture |
| 1951 | Richmond, VA | Virginia Museum of Fine Arts | Watercolors by Virginia Artists |
| | Lynchburg, VA | Randolph-Macon Art Gallery | Art Faculty in Virginia Colleges |
| 1953 | Lynchburg, VA* | Lynchburg Art Center | Pierre Daura |
| 1955 | Lynchburg, VA* | Lynchburg Art Center | Pierre Daura |
| 1957 | Roanoke, VA* | Roanoke Fine Arts Center | Works of Pierre Daura |
| | Lynchburg, VA | Lynchburg Art Club | Annual Civic Art Show |
| 1959 | Lynchburg, VA* | Lynchburg Art Center | Pierre Daura |
| 1961 | Lexington, VA* | Washington & Lee University | Exhibition of Works by Pierre Daura |
| | Blacksburg, VA* | Blackburg Art Association | Paintings & Sculptures by Pierre Daura |
| 1962 | Lynchburg, VA* | Lynchburg Art Center | Pierre Daura |
| | Roanoke, VA* | Roanoke Fine Arts Center | Pierre Daura |
| | Staunton, VA* | Staunton Art Center | Pierre Daura |
| 1963 | Lynchburg, VA* | Lynchburg Art Center | Pierre Daura Exhibition |
| 1967 | Roanoke, VA* | Roanoke Fine Arts Center | Pierre Daura |
| | Lexington, VA* | Washington & Lee University | Pierre Daura |
| 1968 | Lexington, VA | Virginia Military Institute | Pierre Daura & Marion Junkin |
| 1970 | St. Cirq Lapopie | Musée J. Rignault | Exposition d'Été 70 |
| 1973 | Staunton, VA* | Mary Baldwin College | Pierre Daura. Paintings, Watercolors & Sculptures |
| 1974 | Lynchburg, VA* | Dillard Fine Arts Center, Lynchburg College | Mr. Pierre Daura, an Exhibition of His Works |
| 1977 | Lexington, VA | Virginia Military Institute | A Tribute to Louise Blair Daura and Pierre Daura |
| | Barcelona | Dau al Set | Avantguarda catalana 1916-1936 |
| 1978 | Lynchburg, VA | Lynchburg Fine Art Center | Memorial Exhibition of Louise & Pierre Daura |
| 1979 | Cahors* | Musée de Cahors | Pierre Daura |
| | Lexington, VA | Washington & Lee University | Rockbridge Viewed |
| | Blacksburg, VA* | Virginia Polytechnic Institute-State University | Pierre Daura |

| 1980 | Madrid | Palacio Velázquez | 100 años de cultura catalana |
|------|--------|-------------------|------------------------------|
| | Barcelona | Dau al Set | Col·lecció Dau al Set |
| 1985 | Lynchburg, VA | E.C. Glass High School | E.C. Glass Art Collection |
| 1989 | Lexington, VA | Rockbridge Historical Society | Points of View Art Show |
| 1990 | Lynchburg, VA* | Daura Gallery, Lynchburg College | A Daura Retrospective |
| 1993 | St. Cirq Lapopie* | Musée Rignault | Retrospective |
| | Funes, Arg. | Banco Independencia | Los Amigos de Cochet |
| 1995 | Montserrat* | Museu de Montserrat | Daura. De la Mediterrània als Apalatxes |
| | Lynchburg, VA* | Daura Gallery, Lynchburg College | Retrospective |
| 1996 | Washington, DC* | French Embassy | Retrospective |
| | Ciutadella* | Museu Diocesà de Menorca | Pere Daura |
| | Cajarc | Maison des Arts Georges Pompidou | Autour de Cercle et Carré |
| 1997 | Perpignan* | Musée Hyacinthe Rigaud | Daura au Musée Hyacinthe Rigaud |
| | Toulouse* | Musée Paul Dupuy | Pierre Daura. Oeuvres sur Papier |
| 1998 | San Antonio, TX* | San Antonio Museum of Art | Pierre Daura and His Art |
| 1999 | Barcelona* | Sala d'Art Artur Ramon | Pere Daura. Anys vint i trenta |
| | Cahors* | Musée Henri Martin | Pierre Daura |
| | Barcelona* | Museu Nacional d'Art de Catalunya | Pere Daura, retorn a Catalunya |

*Solo Exhibitions*

# INDEX OF NAMES

BIBLIOGRAPHY

*Agrupació d'Artistes Catalans*, 1a Exposició, Galeries Dalmau, Barcelona, 1919.

*Agrupació d'Artistes Catalans*, 4a Exposició, Galeries Dalmau, Barcelona, 1925.

Alcantara i Gusart, M., "L'esperit patriòtic del Mediterrani, a proposit de l'exposició de Pere Daura a les Galeries Badrinas", *Gaseta de les Arts*, Barcelona, No. 10, June 1929, pp. 143-144.

Andrenius [Modest Sabaté], "Una conversa amb el pintor Pere Daura", *La Veu de Catalunya*, Barcelona, December 1, 1932.

Aragay, Ignasi, "La filla del pintor Pere Daura i el Museu Nacional d'Art ultimen un acord de donació", *Avui,* Barcelona, May 29, 1994.

"Art Rebels Hold Own Show", *Daily Mail*, November 8, 1928.

Artís-Gener, A., "Adéu elegíac a Ramon Batlle i al seu ofici", *Serra d'Or*, Barcelona, No. 166, July 15, 1973, p. 440.

*Associations Artistiques les Surindépendants*, première exposition, Paris, 1929.

Baiarola, "Pere Daura", *La Veu de Catalunya*, Barcelona, May 29, 1929, p. 4.

*Barcelona-París, 1900-1960. A la recerca de la llibertat.* Dau al Set. Barcelona.

Benejam, Marga, "Inaugurada la sala de pintura Pere Daura en el museo del Seminario Diocesano", *Diario de Menorca*, Ciutadella, July 14, 1996, p. 10.

Benet, R., "Pere Daura a les Galeries Syra", *La Veu de Catalunya*, Barcelona, December 1, 1932, p. 5.

Bénezit, *Dictionaire Critique et Documentaire des Peintres, Sculpteurs, Dessinateurs et Graveurs*, Gründ, Paris, 1976.

Benoit, P.A., *Seuphor, la Traversée du Siècle*, Musée - Bibliothèque P.A. Benoit, Alès, 1991, p. 17.

Breton, André, *L'Art Magique,* Paris, 1957, p. 67.

Cadena, J.M., "Daura, pintor en Virgínia", *Diario de Barcelona*, Barcelona, March 9, 1975.

Cadena, J. M., "Fallecíó en Estados Unidos el pintor catalan Pere Daura", *Diario de Barcelona,* Barcelona, January 10, 1976.

Cadena, J.M., "Daura de los Apalaches", *El Periódico de Cataluña*, Barcelona, July 28, 1995.

Cadena, J.M., "Perfum dels anys 30", *El Periódico de Catalunya*, Barcelona, March 12, 1999.

Capdevila, Carles, "El pintor Pere Daura", *La Publicitat*, Barcelona, December 4, 1932.

Cassanyes, M. A., *Exposición de arte moderno nacional y extranjero*, Galerias Dalmau, Barcelona, 1929.

*5 Peintres Refusés par le Jury du Salon d'Automne*, Galerie Marck, Paris, 1928.

"5 Peintres Refusés par le Jury du Salon d'Automne", *Le Monde*, Paris, November 3, 1928.

"5 Peintres Refusés par le Jury du Salon d'Automne", *Volonté,* Paris, November 3, 1928.

"5 Peintres Refusés par le Jury du Salon d'Automne", *L'Intransigeant,* Paris, November 12, 1928.

Cirlot, Juan Eduardo, *Pintura catalana contemporánea*, Ediciones Omega, Barcelona, 1961, p, 60.

Clivillés, E., "La pintura de Pere Daura", *El Matí*, Barcelona, December 18, 1935.

Clivillés, E., "Pere Daura", *Esplai*, Barcelona, Vol. II, No. 212, December 22, 1935.

Cochet, Gustavo, *Del diario de un pintor*, Conducta, Buenos Aires, 1941.

Colrat, Bernard, "Cinq refusés", *Renaissance*, Paris, November 17, 1928.

Cortès [i Vidal ] Joan, *Setanta anys de vida artística barcelonina* , Editorial Selecta, Barcelona, 1990.

Cruz, Pedro da, *Torres Garcia and Cercle et Carré*, University of Lund, 1994, pp. 74, 102.

C. i V., J., "Pere Daura", *L'Opinió,* Barcelona, December 3, 1932.

*Daura,* "Fundació Paulí Bellet. Butlletí", Associació de catalans de l'Àrea de Washington, No. 27, January, 1996.

Daura, Louise de, "The Soldier Returns. Spanish Letters", *The Atlantic Monthly*, Boston, January, 1938.

"Daura Exhibit Opens Sunday in Lynchburg", *News-Gazette*, Lexington, November 20, 1974.

"El arte y los artistas. Pedro Daura", *Gaceta de Bellas Artes,* No. 418, December, 1932.

"El museu Diocesà inaugura divendres la Sala de pintura Pere Daura", *Diari de Menorca,* Ciutadella, July 11, 1996, p. 12.

"Els cinc refusats al Saló de Tardor de París", *La Publicitat*, Barcelona, November 14, 1928, p. 6.

"Exposició de l'Agrupació d'Artistes Catalans", *Catalunya Gràfica*, Barcelona, No. 5, February 20, 1922.

"Exposició de l'artista català exiliat Pere Daura", *Avui*, Barcelona, July 19, 1995.

"Exposició Pere Daura", *La Publicitat*, Barcelona, June 4, 1929.

Fernández, Àngel, "Carles Albesa", *Mirador*, Barcelona, July 30, 1931, p. 7.

Folch i Torres, Joaquim, "L'exposició de l'Agrupació d'Artistes Catalans", *Gaseta de les Arts*, Barcelona, No. 66, February 1, 1927, p. 6.

Fontbona, Francesc, *El paisatgisme a Catalunya*, Destino, Barcelona, 1979.

Fontbona, Francesc, "Pere Daura i Garcia", *Gran Enciclopèdia Catalana*, Barcelona, Vol. 6, 1974, p. 58.

Frisach, Montse, "El retorn a casa de Pere Daura", *Avui*, Barcelona, February 28, 1999.

Galbraith, Gracious, "One-Man Show at Staunton Fine Arts Center a Success", *Staunton News Leader,* Staunton, April 22, 1962.

"Galeries d'Art. Syra," *La Veu de Catalunya*, Barcelona, November 3, 1932, p. 4.

"Galeries Syra. Pere Daura", *L'Opinió*, Barcelona, December 3, 1932, p. 8.

Gasch, Sebastià, "Les exposicions", *L'Amic de les Arts*, Sitges, February 28, 1927, p. 17.

Garrut, J.M., *Dos siglos de pintura catalana XIX i XX,* Ibérico Europea de Ediciones, Madrid, 1974.

Gifreda, Màrius, "Pere Daura", *Mirador,* May 30, 1929, p.7.

Gifreda, Màrius, "Exposicions. Pere Daura", *Mirador*, Barcelona, August 13, 1931, p.7.

Gifreda, Màrius, "Exposició d'Art Modern Nacional i Estranger", *Mirador*, Barcelona, November 11, 1929, p. 7.

Gifreda, Màrius, "Les exposicions. Pere Daura", *Mirador*, Barcelona, December 8, 1932, p. 7.

Gifreda, Màrius, *La Veu de Catalunya*, Barcelona, December 7, 1932.

Gifreda, Màrius, *Mirador*, Barcelona, June 13, 1933, p. 7.

Gual, Enric F., "Saló de Montjuïc", *Mirador,* Barcelona, June 8, 1933, p. 7.

Gual, Enric F., "Pere Daura", *Mirador*, Barcelona, December 26, 1935, p. 8.

Hammersley, Howard, "Artist Daura Emphasizes Moods in Experimental Study", *The Roanoke Times*, Roanoke, November 25, 1951.

Jardí, Enric, *Torres García*, Polígrafa, Barcelona, 1973.

Jardí, Enric, *Els moviments d'avantguarda a Barcelona*, Edicions del Cotal s.a., Barcelona, 1983.

Jardí, Enric, (Coord.) *L'Art Català Contemporani*, Proa, Barcelona, 1972.

Kaeppelin, Olivier, *Autour de Cercle et Carré, pour Pierre Daura et Joaquin Torres-García*, Maison des Arts Georges Pompidou, Cajarc, September 15 - November 3, 1996.

Laplana, Josep de C., "Pere Daura. De la Mediterrània als Apalatxes", *Serra d'Or*, Barcelona, No. 436, April, 1996, pp. 284-286

Laurant, Darrel, "Pierre Daura", *The News & Advance*, Lynchburg, January 14, 1996.

Laurant, Darrel, "A Diverse Trio Looks at Daura", *The News & Advance*, Lynchburg, March 30, 1997.

Leon-Martin, Louis, "Les Refusés", *Paris Soir*, Paris, November, 1928.

"Les exposicions. Pere Daura", *Mirador*, Barcelona, December 7, 1933, p. 7.

"Les Refusés", *Le Cri du Jour*, Paris, November 22, 1928.

*Les Surindépendants*, Première exposition, Porte de Versailles - Parc des Expositions, Paris, 1929.

Macià, Teresa, "Pere Daura (1896-1976). Una trajectòria artística entre Catalunya, França i Virgínia", *Pere Daura. Anys vint i trenta*, Sala d'Art Artur Ramon, Barcelona, February - April 1999.

Maragall, Joan A., *Història de la Sala Parès*, Editorial Selecta, Barcelona, 1975.

Mates, Joan, "Pere Daura a Saint Cirq", *Art*, Barcelona, Vol. 1, 1933 - 1934, pp. 177-182.

Merli, Joan, *33 pintors catalans*, Barcelona, 1976, pp. 63-68. (1st edition, Barcelona, 1937)

Miralles, Francesc, "L'època de les avantguardes 1917-1970", *Història de l'Art Català*, Edicions 62, Barcelona, Vol. 8, 1983.

Miralles, Francesc, "Un nómada catalán", *La Vanguardia*, Barcelona, March 26, 1999.

"Mrs. Louise Blair Daura", *The Daily Advance*, November 14, 1972.

Montserrat, Daniel, "Conversa amb el pintor Pere Daura, un dels catalans refusats al Saló de Tardor de París", *La Nau*, Barcelona, January 26, 1929.

"Montserrat recupera l'oblidat Daura", *Regió 7*, Manresa, July 20, 1995, p. 39.

"Montserrat vist pels artistes catalans. Els cinc grans premis de pintura del concurs", "*La Veu de Catalunya*", Barcelona, October 24, 1931.

Munger, Robert S., "Daura Exhibition Proves Artist's Strength, Versatility" *Rockbridge County News*, Lexington, January 12, 1961.

"Organitzacions i Galeries d'Art. Syra. Pere Daura", *La Veu de Catalunya*, Barcelona, November 23, 1932, p. 5.

"París. Una exposición de rebeldes", *Blanco y Negro*, Madrid, December 9, 1928.

Pasamonte, Javier de, "En nombre del padre", *La Vanguardia*, Barcelona, February 27, 1999.

"Pedro Daura", *La Noche*, Barcelona, December 6, 1932.

"Pere Daura," *La Veu de Catalunya*, Barcelona, December 7, 1932, p. 5.

*Pierre Daura, Expose*, Galerie René Zivy, Paris, 1928.

"Pierre Daura Finds Medium of Sculpture -Its Paper Pulp", *The News*, Lynchburg, April 19, 1959.

Pons, Josep, "Obre el Museu Diocesà de Menorca amb un varietat d'exposicions", *Avui*, Barcelona, August 4, 1996.

Prat, Marie-Aline, *Cercle et Carré. Peinture et Avant-garde au Seuil des Années 30*, Seuil, Paris.

Ràfols, J.F., "Pere Daura", *El Matí*, Barcelona, December 8, 1932, p. 9.

Ràfols, J.F., *Diccionario biográfico de artistas de Cataluña*, Editorial Millà, Barcelona, 1951, p. 341.

"Refused by Salon, They Hold Own Show", *Chicago Tribune*, Paris edition, November 25, 1928.

R.V., "Paisatges de Corsega", *El Matí*, Barcelona, May 31, 1929, p. 9.

Sabaté, M., "Exposició Pere Daura a les Galeries Syra", *La Veu del Vespre*, Barcelona, December 13, 1933.

Sabaté, M., "Descoberta del refugi del pintor Pere Daura", *L'Instant*, Barcelona, March 25, 1936.

Santos Torroella, Rafael, "Pere Daura", *El Noticiero Universal*, Barcelona, January 12, 1976.

Sarllès, Y., "Cinq Peintres Refusés au Salon d'Automne Exposent rue Bonaparte Leurs Chefs-d'oeuvre Incompris", *Paris Midi*, Paris, November 7, 1928.

Serra, Catalina, "La operación rescate de Pere Daura", *El País*, Barcelona, February 24, 1999.

Seuphor, Michel, *Le Style et le Cri*, Seuil, Paris, 1965.

Sheck, Ken, "Pierre Daura Recalled at Gallery Dedication", *The News-Gazette*, Lexington, November 1, 1995.

Torres-García, Joaquín, *Historia de mi vida*, Paidós, Barcelona - Buenos Aires - México, 1990. (1st edition, Montevideo, 1939).

Torres-García, J., "Pere Daura", *La Veu de Catalunya*, Barcelona, June 22, 1929.

Trenc, Eliseu, "Cercle et Carré", *Avui*, Barcelona, November 14, 1996.

"Tres jóvenes artistas", *La Publicitat*, Barcelona, November 23, 1911.

Viatte, G., *Seuphor,* Fons Mercator, Anvers, 1976.

Valaison, M.C., *Daura au Musée Hyacinthe Rigaud,* Musée Hyacinthe Rigaud, Perpignan, 1997.

Valaison, M.C., "Un Legs et Une Donation pour le Musée Rigaud", *Perpignan Magazine*, Perpignan, No. 11, Christmas 1995, p. 26.

Vélez, Pilar, "La donació Daura a Montserrat", *Avui*, Barcelona, September 7, 1995.

Vélez, Pilar, "La redescoberta de Pere Daura (1896-1976)", *Avui*, Barcelona, April 15, 1999.

Vidal, Jaume, "El Museo de Montserrat recupera la obra y memoria del pintor catalan Pere Daura", *El País*, Barcelona, July 20, 1995.

Wiley, Lib, "Art Gallery Picks Pierre Daura for First One-Man Exhibition", *The Advance*, Lynchburg, October 30, 1953.

Xceron, John, "Pierre Daura", *Chicago Tribune*, Paris edition, 1929, p. 4.

Young, Priscilla, "Pierre Daura and To Man, Compassion", *The Roanoke Times*, Roanoke, January 8, 1961.

Young, Priscilla, "Pierre Daura's Work on Display", *The Roanoke Times*, Roanoke, October 28, 1962.